# THE
# ORAL STUDY
# OF
# LITERATURE

# STUDIES IN SPEECH

CONSULTING EDITOR: *Don Geiger*

UNIVERSITY OF CALIFORNIA, BERKELEY

# THE
# ORAL STUDY
# OF
# LITERATURE

*Robert Beloof / Chester Clayton Long*
*Seymour Chatman*
*Thomas O. Sloan / Mark S. Klyn*

EDITED WITH AN INTRODUCTION BY
THOMAS O. SLOAN

RANDOM HOUSE / NEW YORK

807
SL50

First Printing

© Copyright, 1966, by Random House, Inc.

Library of Congress Catalog Card Number: 66–11149

Manufactured in the United States of America
by H. Wolff, New York

67504

## ACKNOWLEDGMENTS

October 1969

Acknowledgments are gratefully extended to the following authors and publishers for their kind permission to quote from copyrighted material.

Herbert C. Barrows, Jr., and William R. Steinhoff, "Cummings' ANYONE LIVED IN A PRETTY HOW TOWN," from *The Explicator,* IX (Oct. 1950), #1. Copyright 1950 by *The Explicator.* By permission of the publisher and authors.

Arthur J. Carr, "Cummings' ANYONE LIVED IN A PRETTY HOW TOWN," from *The Explicator,* XI (Nov. 1952), #6. Copyright 1952 by *The Explicator.* By permission of the publisher and author.

Anton Chekhov, "Ward No. 6," from *Seven Short Novels of Chekhov,* trans. Barbara Makanowitzky. Copyright © 1963 by Bantam Books, Inc. By permission of the publisher.

Anton Chekhov, *Letters of Anton Chekhov to His Family and Friends,* ed. and trans. Constance Garnett. Copyright 1920 by The Macmillan Company; Renewed 1948 by David Garnett. Reprinted by permission of The Macmillan Company and Chatto and Windus Ltd.

Robert Frost, "Dust of Snow," from *Complete Poems of Robert Frost.* Copyright 1923 by Holt, Rinehart and Winston, Inc. Copyright 1951 by Robert Frost. Reprinted by permission of Holt, Rinehart and Winston, Inc.

Robert Lowell, "Where the Rainbow Ends," from *Lord Weary's*

# PREFACE

This book was written first as an aid to the student studying literature from the standpoint of its re-creation in speech. His study is usually named "oral interpretation" or simply "interpretation." The interpretation student needs a variety of critical analyses, tools, and strategies which he may combine with oral performance in his study of literature. This book was written to help meet that need.

But it was written also as a kind of apologetic, aimed particularly at the student who is interested in studying literature but is uncertain of the role played by oral performance in that study. To our grandfathers, interpretation was "elocution," primarily a subject that taught students how to execute vocal and physical gymnastics in the recitation of literature—an execution that literature managed, somehow, to survive. To our fathers, interpretation was usually a course that stressed the culture of voice and gesture and was important mostly because it led to the more clearly practical art of public speaking or the more clearly defined art of acting. This book was written as part of the continuing effort in our field to demonstrate the relevance of interpretation to the critical study of literature.

Finally, this book was written for the "general" student, too, that sometimes rare species who uses time on campus to satisfy curiosity about a great number of subjects. The "general" student might wish to know what some people find so fascinating about, of all things, literary criticism. Undoubtedly he has heard our age called an Age of Criticism and an Age of Anxiety, and he may wonder if there is some connection between the two. There may be. Anyone who has already discovered how to read literature is bound to become anxious when he finds students flocking to observe the whirligig motions of literary criticism while only a few students seem interested in, or even capable of, contemplating the workings of literature itself. Our book may show why, as teachers of interpretation and as students of literature, we continue to be enthusiastic about certain developments in literary criticism.

The title of our book was first used more than forty years ago by Algernon Tassin, who believed that reading aloud well is not only a test of apprehension but also a means of learning the principles of literary criticism through concrete application (*The Oral Study of Literature,* New York: Alfred A. Knopf, Inc., 1923). His title is the shortest expression of the central principle on which our book is based: *the proper application of oral interpretation is as a discipline through which the student engages in the study of literature.* Utilizing that principle, this book attempts to show the relationship between literary criticism and performance problems in oral interpretation and to show that *together* critical analysis and oral performance provide a sure foundation for literary study.

This book bears important relationships to certain modern books in the field of oral interpretation, especially to Don Geiger's *The Sound, Sense, and Performance of Literature* (Chicago: Scott, Foresman, 1963). Geiger's definition of oral interpretation and his discussion of the dramatic analysis of literature are particularly useful points of reference for our concerns in this volume. Unlike our book, Geiger's discusses in depth the literary identity of oral interpretation, its nature and rationale. Unlike Geiger's, our book utilizes this identity in the analysis of literature through five critical methods.

For the student interested in exploring our subjects further, we have included brief materials for additional study at the end of each chapter. The student will also need to obtain copies, where they are not included in the text, of the poems, stories, plays, and recordings referred to throughout this book. He will benefit by reading the critical works referred to in our discussions. Above all, he will benefit by the help in literary analysis and speech skills that can be provided only by the teacher in the classroom.

T.O.S.

*Urbana, Illinois*
*July, 1965*

# CONTENTS

# THE
# ORAL STUDY
# OF
# LITERATURE

# INTRODUCTION

Oral interpretation, the oral study of literature, is a discipline which endeavors to bring together the activities of speaking the poem and of speaking *about* the poem, in the belief that together these activities answer the challenge of *reading* the poem. To introduce theoretically the values of this study, let us review the recent history of the change, in our field, from elocution to interpretation. We shall find that the change developed along with forces at work elsewhere in literary study—forces that gathered in response to one of the great challenges hurled at educators in the beginning of our century: the need to train readers not merely to understand what they are reading but to enter deeply into the life of literature.

In our field, these forces produced a change in methods for achieving that goal. Actually, though its emphasis on methods has sometimes obscured its goal, the theory and practice of performing literature orally have *always* been

3

aimed at increasing literary understanding both in the audience and in the performer. That goal appeared in the charges which Socrates leveled at the hapless rhapsode Ion, who could only rest his case for interpretational excellence on inspiration. It appeared in the writings of the sixteenth-century English schoolmaster who made his boys read Virgil aloud to see if they had acquired anything more than accurate pronunciation of Latin words. It appeared in the intellectual ferment that two centuries ago gave birth to the elocutionary movement.

The elocutionary movement began in the eighteenth century as an attempt, in part, to make a systematic study of oral delivery. Such a study had clear implications for the student of literature, but its emphasis on methods was underscored by its stated goal of improving the professional training of *all* speakers. By the nineteenth century, study had largely given way to system. The effort of many elocutionists was aimed at producing manuals of gestures, books of pictures showing the proper posturing for each emotion. One such book has, among its many illustrations, a picture of a rather large woman, in long skirt and leg-o'-mutton sleeves, leaning forward on her downstage foot, shading her eyes with her right hand, her left arm stretched toward the upstage area, her eyes straining toward something off-stage right. The emotion she is expressing, according to the caption, is "discernment." To study a poem by the method outlined in that book, one first identified the emotions in the poem (how one was meant to do this is never spelled out), found the postures representing these emotions, then assumed the postures as he recited the poem aloud. Though the elocutionists' view of emotion was ludicrously simple, there can be no question that they were fantastically successful in appealing to an age of bric-a-brac and virtu.

In 1903, an Englishman who was a devotee of the art of elocution requested popular reciters to send him copies of their favorite selections. He wanted to preserve in book form mementos of an art that he sadly realized was dying. In his preface he reports:

> That charming and gifted elocutionist, Mrs. Brown-Potter, sends us a rich and varied choice of "favourite" subjects for recitation. It will be perceived that Mrs. Potter includes Tennyson's ever-green but immortal "Charge of the Light Brigade," which she does, in fact, recite very beautifully and artistically. Tennyson is a favourite poet of hers, and at midnight on the New Year's eve of 1901–2 she did a characteristically poetic thing, reciting his "Ring Out Wild Bells," out of *In Memoriam,* in the belfry of Gorleston Church, at the invitation of the Mayor and Corporation.[1]

As the Mayor, Corporation, and townsfolk stood in the shattered calm of that New Year's morn, perhaps neither they nor Mrs. Brown-Potter could believe that the wild bells would soon be ringing out elocution with the old— the old and very inadequate.

Little wonder that elocution had no future. A discriminating member of the audience would have known that genuine literature, such as *In Memoriam,* is far richer than it appeared through the elocutionist's delivery. And if what the elocutionist did really was the "characteristically poetic thing," it would have been unlikely that poetry itself could have survived the intellectual revolutions at the beginning of our century.

Early in our century, a few men—notably S. S. Curry and Solomon Henry Clark—realized that elocution had side-tracked us from the true course of our study. That course runs on the principle that delivery and understanding do not merely go hand-in-hand, as the elocutionists professed to believe, but that the two stand in a much more complicated reciprocal relationship than the elocutionists had ever dreamed possible. With that realization, the modern character of our study was born, and its alliance with the forces shaping modern literary criticism was inevitable. The name "elocution" was dropped, and the new character of the study was displayed in the names "literary interpretation," "oral interpretation of literature," or simply "interpretation."

At about the time that this realization began to hasten the fading of elocution, a complementary force began changing the character of literary criticism. In the first two decades of this century, certain literary critics started to express dissatisfaction with earlier approaches to literature. These critics believed that in literature words take on a peculiarly complex meaning and that the proper study of literature focuses on that peculiarly complex meaning. "The poem means what it says," according to these critics. Therefore, the words of the poem itself should be studied carefully in terms of the context, the permissible range of denotations and connotations, rather than in terms of the poet's life and times. Styling themselves "New Critics" and vigorously defending their "intrinsic" approach to literature, they began to restructure literary studies in the 1930's.

But in the art of interpretation, the same doctrine was already at work. As far back as 1923, Algernon Tassin had written an interpretation textbook entitled *The Oral Study of Literature* whose purpose was to encourage the use of oral reading in literary study.[2] It fused the process of good oral reading with painstaking verbal analysis of literature and, thus, accorded well with the close-reading-of-the-words-themselves emphasis in New Criticism. Tassin saw oral reading as an instrument—both a pedagogical and a critical instrument—useful in all respects and necessary in some, for the intrinsic approach to the study of literature. His work went through five editions, the last one in 1947.

Tassin's mode of analysis will not seem to us, in the perspective of modern developments in literary and oral interpretation theory, as efficient as our own. Yet his work stands as a clear example, certainly not the first, and hardly the last, of the continuing attempt to align the discipline of oral reading with ongoing developments in educational and literary theory. The alignment with New-Critical developments became complete when interpretation theorists began using the argument that if the poem means what it says, then a good way to understand and share that meaning must lie in the attempt to say the poem.

One doctrine in recent criticism that has particularly attracted interpretation theorists is that literary meaning is not so much discursive as dramatic.[3] By this doctrine, meaning should be grasped not merely in terms of denotation and connotation but also in terms of speaker, situation, and action. Meaning is, in short, what "happens" in literature. The "happening" is typically a speaker responding to or within a situation. Maybe he is experiencing sorrow because of his age or because of his youth; maybe he is experiencing anger at someone or something within his situation, or regret that there is no one or nothing within his situation. At any rate, meaning emerges through words, movement, gesture, the character of the speaker, and the nature of his situation. It cannot be expressed as a statement, as a theme, or even as a paraphrase. It can be partially expressed by critical talk about the literature. But it can be more than partially expressed by the oral interpreter who, with the language of the literature itself, *performs* the "happening."

The doctrine further holds that we go to literature in order to experience the responses that are stimulated by our imaginative observance of, or participation in, these "happenings." The situations in literature rarely include us. We make ourselves a part of the situations by allowing our imagination to be engaged. This we do through a knowledge based on our past experience with the art of literature, whereby we have learned that if we will willingly join in the already-created situations we will observe or even virtually take part in a "happening" that may be probable or believable. We prove the "truth" of literature both in our minds and, in the rhetorician's phrase, "on our pulses" as we make the full sum of responses which a sensitive reader can undergo when he opens to himself the situations in literature. Because the enjoyment of literature demands this full engagement, it has continued to be an important part of living. Because interpretation, too, demands this full engagement, it has continued to be an important pedagogical and critical instrument for studying literature. Unlike the silent student of literature, the oral interpreter seeks overtly to translate his engagement into vocal and bodily behavior, thereby sharpening his own engagement and encouraging his audience's empathic responses.

Thus, literature is seen, in terms of speaker-situation-action, as a "dramatic use of language." The interpreter applying this view has a basic set of questions to ask: Who is speaking? To whom? What does he say? Why? How? Where? When? In performing the literature—even performing for himself alone—he answers the most important question, so far as "meaning" is concerned: How do the answers to these questions relate to one another? Unlike all other students of literature, the oral interpreter answers these questions simultaneously, through his performance. His performance is an attempt to make literature dramatically intelligible and thereby to call forth from himself and from his audience the sort of response which literature can stimulate.

Interpretation, then, seen as the modern oral study of literature, means two things. For the oral interpreter, it means the utilization of the dramatic view of literature, a view that encompasses all the five analyses presented in this book. The oral interpreter is faced with the task of making literature dramatically intelligible, to himself and to his audience, and all his critical activities are aimed at accomplishing that task. For him, analyzing a selection becomes fused with rehearsing it for oral performance. For the audience, the oral performance itself can be a "study" if the audience regards the reading not merely as a form of amusement but primarily as an illumination of literature, a rendering offered publicly in the way a critical essay is offered, to share an insight into the "happenings" in literature. Ideally, the audience studies the oral reading in terms of what it knows about the literature and the literature in terms of what it knows about the oral reading. Insofar as the interpreter makes himself a member of his own audience, his public performance continues his study.

Let us conclude this discussion of the literary bearings of modern interpretation by viewing interpretation as a speech art. In all the modern speech arts, good delivery is usually defined as that which flows from and reveals the speaker's "vivid realization of meaning at the moment of utterance." "Meaning," of course, is involved not only in what words *say* but also in what they *do,* their effect upon speaker and audience; in each speech art, delivery varies as meaning varies, that is, as the nature of the discourse studied varies. Interpretation, as we see it, studies literature through oral performances evoked by what the words in literature say and do. Thus, oral performance is a critical instrument, for it presents a structure of meaning that is a basis for further investigation, and it is a pedagogical instrument, for it demonstrates both the student's grasp of meaning and his ability to convey it orally.

Let us turn now to the task assumed by this book. The interpreter's dramatic view provides a framework for our critical principles. Although our closest allies in recent history have been the New Critics, we have not limited our analyses to their intrinsic approach. The following chapters attempt to show how the oral interpreter may utilize within his dramatic view the extrinsic as well as the intrinsic approach to literature. All within the framework of the dramatic view of literature, we shall present three analyses utilizing the intrinsic approach and two utilizing the extrinsic.

Our first analysis, the explicative, is most fundamentally intrinsic in its approach. Having been given great prominence in our day by the New Critics, explication attempts basically to study how the words in a literary text acquire meaning and function within the larger structure of that text and to make this study with a minimum of help external to the reader-text relationship. However, thirty years of explicative analysis have shown that all critics, regardless of how "new" they are, have *some* outside help. The critic brings to his task some basic concept which forms the framework for his investigations. The framework fundamental to the explicative as well as to all the other analyses in this book is that provided by the dramatic concept of literary meaning. As employed in our first analysis, the concept offers important safeguards against misusing the explicative analysis and even against committing the errors made by early New Critics in applying the explicative analysis within narrowly-conceived boundaries of the intrinsic approach. The operation of this concept provides similar safeguards in the other analyses in this book.

Our second analysis, the formal, is, like the explicative, intrinsic. As its name implies, its center of interest is form, the order the writer has given to his materials. Explication begins the job; but whereas the explicator limits himself to the details of the poem, formal analysis seeks to place the total, organic action of the poem among other kinds of action. If the explicator is the psychoanalyst of the poem, the formalist is its sociologist—he wants to see it finally in its place among other related works and to see clearly its uniqueness.

Utilizing knowledge gained through modern attempts to objectify language phenomena, the linguistic analysis offers a clear connection between literary text and oral performance; for linguistics offers us a way to specify some of those aspects of delivery—usually the vocal ones—fundamental to the oral study of literature. And, like the oral interpreter, the linguist is concerned with a view of the poem as an oral construct, something to be studied within the possibilities of oral delivery. As used in this book, the linguistic analysis is the third type of intrinsic approach.

The last two chapters of this book approach literature from increasingly extrinsic points of view. The rhetorical analysis studies possible strategies of persuasion in literary structures. The final chapter, employing a biographical-social analysis, thinks of the work as the writer's response to his own milieu. The differences, in method and in attitude, between the last two analyses are subtle: one analysis focuses on the writer's audience and his ostensible strategies for engaging his audience; the other focuses on the writer's struggles to achieve artistic integrity out of his response to his life and times.

But the differences between all of the analyses are subtle compared with the intrinsic-extrinsic division in approaches. The first three analyses use for their critical method primarily that information which may be immediately available to any reader of the work; the last two employ information which is not always immediately available but which must be sought through research into matters which exist outside the text of the work itself. The oral interpreter should employ whatever approach or whatever analysis "works"—and that will depend on how much he believes he has learned about the nature of his selection and about his task as oral performer of that selection. Literature is too varied and the oral performance of literature too complex to require that either be approached within restrictive categories. Thus, though there is a single major division in this book, no difference, however slight, between these analyses and the role each constructs for the oral interpreter should be overlooked—for each difference attests to the diversity possible within the dramatic view of literary meaning. Many of our analyses are clearly unorthodox, but we have not consciously tried to be either provocative or provoking; however, in order to say what we have wanted to say and to say it forcibly, we have found it necessary at times to clash not only with certain literary critics and oral interpretation theorists but also with each other. Safeguards provided by the dramatic view, important though they are for preventing insularity, limit neither the applicability of any critical analysis nor its potential for controversy.

The modern oral study of literature is the result of several forces which were at work at the beginning of this century. In the field of speech these forces produced the change from elocution to interpretation, and in the field of literary criticism they produced the change from predominantly biographical and social approaches to the New-Critical intrinsic approach and even beyond to the dramatic concept of literary meaning. Our task in this book is neither to spur those changes nor to start new ones. Our task, rather, is to present five diverse analytical methods within a commonly-shared perspective, in the hopes that these methods will help readers become more adept at experiencing those actions and voices which for centuries it has been the unique role of literature to present.

NOTES

1. Percy Cross' Standing, ed., *Favourite Recitations of Favourite Actors* (London: T.C. and E.C. Jack, 1903), p. vii.
2. Algernon Tassin, *The Oral Study of Literature* (New York: Alfred A. Knopf, Inc., 1923).

3. The dramatic view sketched here is explored in some depth in its relations to oral interpretation by Wallace A. Bacon and Robert S. Breen, *Literature as Experience* (New York: McGraw-Hill Book Co., 1959) and Don Geiger, *The Sound, Sense, and Performance of Literature* (Chicago: Scott, Foresman, 1963).

# PART I

---

*The*
*Intrinsic Approach*

# CHAPTER ONE

# EXPLICATIVE ANALYSIS:
## A Reading of Robert Lowell's "Where the Rainbow Ends"

*ROBERT BELOOF*

# I

The explicator tries to elucidate the literary work in terms of itself. He wishes to clarify the work's significance by a close look at its parts and their internal relationships. Strictly speaking, of course, this cannot be done, since the work's connections with the larger world are immediately apparent. Indeed, experience of the last twenty years has demonstrated that without a knowledgeable attention to the work's tradition, to the author's canon, his sources, his place in a given society, some pretty egregious misreadings can be committed to print. Nonetheless, the effort remains especially worthwhile for the student—and a necessity for certain works of art in any hand.

In a certain sense, all explications lead to oral interpretation. Or, to put it another way, oral interpretation is the ultimate test for any explication, since any explication should be comprehensible in an oral re-creation of the intonations, pauses, emotional sets—in short, the sequence of tones which will embody its elucidation of the literary work's meaning. Certainly an oral interpretation should stem from an explication, for a proper transformation of the dead words on the page into a passionate commitment of voice and body must rest on a detailed understanding of the work of art as its parts inform and modify each other into a unique sequence of tones. I hope to demonstrate this relationship in the process of taking a close look at Robert Lowell's poem, "Where the Rainbow Ends." But first I think it would be useful to make some comments concerning certain special explicative problems, which are frequently encountered and easily distinguished, and then to discuss some common ways in which explications can go wrong.

It has been pointed out more than once that the advent of the New Criticism (the scholarly movement that first brought *explication de texte* onto center stage in this country) carried with it a shift of taste toward complex poetry. Such poets as Herrick or Burns, among whose chief techniques are clarity of theme and apparent simplicity of means, obviously offer little to the explicator. And there is little doubt that one of the pernicious effects of the new emphasis on close critical reading has been to delude weak heads into a more than occasional insistence that a given simple poem is in fact not simple at all, but complex—an error in taste and literary judgment often compounded by the indefensible assumption that, because it is more complex than had been thought, it is therefore more profound.

I think the act of explication can be saved from this fatal fascination with complexity only if it rejects self-serving ingenuity and scholarly athleticism for a procedure which takes as its goal the comprehension of the proper distance, or the proper perspective, from which to view the work of art. We may conceive of this procedure as arriving at the proper comprehension of tone, a goal which may be achieved with greater speed if one can recognize some of the more common kinds of explicative problems.

1. *The Old Work.* In some cases, a new interpretation arising from the sensibilities of a new age gives fresh insight to an old masterpiece. An example is Simone Weil's essay *The Iliad; or, The Poem of Force.*[1] An even better example might be the Freudian interpretation of Hamlet first advanced in detail by Ernest Jones, the eminent Freudian psychoanalyst.[2] Such explications are likely to seem out of balance, invested with the special interests of a special time. Nonetheless, they seldom leave our view of a work unchanged. We may not believe that the reason for Hamlet's reluctance to act is solely, or even primarily, founded on an Oedipal ambivalence toward his father, but the Freudian insight tells us things about the closet scene which we will not forget.

Sometimes the new explication of a very old work can arise from a reconsideration of some fact or facts concerning the poem's origins. Thus, with the famous old four-line poem "Western Wind When Wilt Thou Blow," a recent critic, by ignoring modern texts and returning to the original manuscript, has given a new interpretation.

*Modern Text*

O western wind, when wilt thou blow
    That the small rain down can rain?
Christ that my love were in my arms
    And I in my bed again.

*Original Text*

Westron Wynde When Wyll Thow blowe
The smalle rayne downe can rayne.
Cryst yf my love were in my Armys
And I yn my bed A gayne.[3]

Based on the modern text, the usual explications make a parallel of the first two and the second two lines, a parallel drawn in the form of an implied figure of speech. Thus, the first two lines are seen as an appeal for the wind that will bring the drought-ending rain. This appeal is the parallel figure illustrating and defining the depth of the lover's need for his loved one, from whom he has presumably been separated.

The above-mentioned explicator,[4] studying the original manuscript version, has speculated that "all previous interpreters of this poem . . . have depended on a corrupt text, in which the spelling is modernized (eliminating all warning that the language may not be equally up-to-date), the punctuation is entirely editorial, and an interpolated word, *that,* appears at the beginning of line 2." This explicator offers a substantially different reading, based primarily on an elimination of the interpolated *that,* on noting that the word "can" in Middle English was a familiar variant of *gan* (from *ginne*) usually meaning "did," and on reminding us that in England the west wind is the wind for fair weather.

Developing these new points, the interpreter suggests that the relation between the first and second pair of lines is quite different from previous interpretations and really represents the lover in the gloom of a rainy day wishing for fair weather, just as he wishes he were in his lover's arms again, though quite unable to hasten either event. So the critic reminds us that with essential aspects lost or ignored in the passage of time, new and sometimes erroneous explications are very likely to arise around old works.

2. *The New Work.* For just the opposite reasons, explications are often useful with new works. Browning's poems, which on the whole present little difficulty to us, were very often puzzling to his contemporaries, and numerous Browning societies sprang up to promote their discussion and elucidation. T. S. Eliot's *The Waste Land,* upon its appearance, required considerable explication for many people. In prose, such a novel as Joyce's *Finnegan's Wake*

is inaccessible even to the sophisticated reader without a complex apparatus of explication.

3. *The Puzzle Poem.* Yet a third kind of poem which invites explication is what I shall call the *puzzle poem.* This is a poem which a very brief explication may open up, since once the key is provided the central meaning of the poem is clear. Such a poem is E. A. Robinson's "How Annandale Went Out."

> "They called it Annandale—and I was there
> To flourish, to find words, and to attend:
> Liar, physician, hypocrite, and friend,
> I watched him; and the sight was not so fair
> As one or two that I have seen elsewhere:
> An apparatus not for me to mend—
> A wreck, with hell between him and the end,
> Remained of Annandale; and I was there.
>
> "I knew the ruin as I knew the man;
> So put the two together, if you can,
> Remembering the worst you know of me.
> Now view yourself as I was, on the spot—
> With a slight kind of engine. Do you see?
> Like this . . . You wouldn't hang me? I thought not." [5]

With this poem a considerable initial difficulty is eliminated by the explanation that the speaker in the poem is a physician, explaining his motivation in performing a mercy killing. Once this essentially dramatic problem of the nature of the speaker is solved, the poem presents little further difficulty.

4. *The Referential (or Allusive) Work.* Here the difficulty requiring explication centers around references or allusions which might be missed by the general audience, or, indeed, by a more specialized reader. Sometimes the references are taken from books or events which were or have become obscure to the general public, and hence are famil-

iar only to the specialist. An excellent example might be Eliot's use of Weston's *From Ritual to Romance* in *The Waste Land.* Or one might mention Swift's *Gulliver's Travels,* whose references to contemporary politics must now partly be seen as a form of a temporal problem (old work).

The second kind of allusion which may require explication is that in which the author invents, as it were, his own references. Thus, when Yeats speaks in his poem "The Tower" of Hanrahan, he is referring to a character he himself created in an early series of stories. In fact, Yeats or Blake can be seen as examples of writers whose world of private references is often primarily a symbolic construct.

5. *The Symbolic Work.* Symbolic works are notorious for the fact that they breed explications—often conflicting ones. But I should like to make some elementary distinctions among symbolic works—distinctions which I hope might help the explicator avoid certain common errors. Many symbolic poems actually arise out of a rich web of imagistic and dramatistic detail. It makes considerable difference whether or not this detail is fantastic or realistic or somewhere in between. Let me be more precise. Poe's "The House of Usher" is fantastic. The tarn, the castle, the characters, are never meant to be taken as anything else. On the other hand Melville's *Moby Dick,* a highly symbolic (allegorical, to be more precise) novel, is literally built like a coral reef of thousands of concrete, realistic details relating to the life of New England whaling. Kafka's work often exists somewhere between. "The Penal Colony" is fantastic, but the detail is in a sense realistic. That is, the machine and the characters are all given in detail, and one is convinced they *could* exist. Perhaps "Metamorphosis" is a better example. Here a young man turns into a very realistic and believable bug.

I have mentioned the allegory as one of the distinct varieties of symbolic works. (Allegories occur sometimes in the most surprising places. E. E. Cummings, though not particularly known as an allegorist, has written some of the best in modern poetry.) There is another type less generally recognized and therefore more frequently misconstrued in explication. This is what I call the "archetypal" poem or story. Here the idea is to present in some ideal or permanently valid form a classic *event* of human existence. The archetypal poem does not seek to explore the individual psyche in terms of a unique event. Rather, it chooses to describe a *pattern* of event which will occur again and again in human experiences in a great variety of realistic circumstances. Walter de la Mare's well-known poem "The Listeners" is an example. Many critics have tried to identify the listeners or the traveler, or even to guess the locale of the poem. These are misguided efforts, for it seems fairly clear that this poem is about man's experience of unreality, of futility, as he acts out the common attempt to return to the past. The poem is in a sense an archetypal pattern of all such efforts, and it is meant to convey a general insight or acquaintance with their mode and mood.

These special problems may or may not be encountered by the student in the particular work he has chosen. Unlike the professional critic who might find that such difficulties would especially reward his attention, the student is attempting to master the tonal detail of a work whose overall thematic meaning may offer little or no difficulty. The point for the student is to see if he has it in himself to achieve this mastery. The poem explicated later in this chapter presents some of the difficulties of a "new" work, in which problems of local reference, literary allusion, and syntax are at the root of its difficulties. Nonetheless, the explication is intended to serve as an example of the "intrinsic" type in its aims and execution, the type the student most frequently encounters in the classroom.

The question arises, does explication develop any distinguishing characteristics in the hands of the oral interpretation student? It is my opinion that it does. These distinguishing characteristics arise from the simple fact that ultimately the explication is part of the preparation for a spoken re-creation of the poem. The interpreter cannot ignore any of the elements of a poem which the student in the mute literature class will note: imagery, figures, theme, diction, meter. But he is forced to see them in a somewhat different light because they must function in such a way as to become transformed for him into specific vocal intonations and bodily reactions. This requirement will also lead him to discuss in detail elements which the student in the mute class may ignore or only touch upon: the character of the narrating voice, the dramatic pattern of characters, the spatial relationship of images, the exact nature of abstract and tonal ambiguities, the precise interplay of rhythm with meter, musical devices with rhythm and meter, grammar and syntax with all three, to name but examples that come easily to mind.

Before turning to an explication of Robert Lowell's poem "Where the Rainbow Ends" it might be well to conclude this general discussion with some comments on the common causes of inaccuracy in explications, inaccuracies leading to improper readings.

As I noted earlier, coming to a firm understanding of a poem has much to do with the ability to keep an overall perspective in one's head while working on details. It is very common to get so involved with a detail that the poem is seen in a way which is completely ruled out by the nature of the whole. As the blind man who felt the tail of the elephant and declared that the elephant was much like a rope, so the critic can see a certain event or relationship and in effect declare it to be the whole poem. Similarly, he can be so in search of deeper meanings that he can, in that search, betray the whole. There is nothing so plain that a closer look at its parts will not reveal new detail and shifting perspectives. Gulliver found the Brobdingnagian giants hideous. Brought close to their faces, he saw their skin pores as great greasy pits, their breath as a nauseous hot gale. Again, any painting will disappear into blobs of color at too great a distance, or dissolve into brush strokes at too near a perspective. There is a proper perspective for viewing a work of literary art which must not be forgotten when bringing it up closer to inspect details. A plain poem is not to be made into a mystery because of the power of the English language for extended meanings, nor is a complex poem to be reduced to simplicity because its theme can be stated in a sentence.

Robert Frost's poem "Dust of Snow" is a very simple poem telling of a simple incident. One evening when Robert Frost was addressing a university audience, a young assistant professor with a career to make arose in the question period and asked Mr. Frost if this poem were not about death. Here is the poem.

> The way a crow
> Shook down on me
> The dust of snow
> From a hemlock tree
>
> Has given my heart
> A change of mood
> And saved some part
> Of a day I had rued.[6]

While Mr. Frost looked absolutely stunned, the young man proceeded to demonstrate that this poem was permeated with symbolism and was basically about death. He pointed out that after all a crow is black and is often in literature connected with death, as is the hemlock. Also, snow is frozen, sterile, overtones which are heightened by calling the snow "dust," thus bringing to mind such phrases as "dust to dust." Apart from demonstrating that the absence of a sense of humor is probably as fatal a flaw as a reader of literature can have, this explication is an excellent example of what horrors can be committed if the parts are looked at out of perspective. This little poem has the wry and casual tone appropriate to a realistic small incident. It contains, in a lovely black-and-white scene, a moment out of nature which reaches across to touch the man in his withdrawn mood—and that is all.

Somewhat similar but not identical is the error of misreading a key detail. An ubiquitous example is the misreading of the Frost poem "Mending Wall," in which the line "Good fences make good neighbors" is taken as the statement of the poet—as expressive of his point of view in the poem. So general is this misunderstanding that *Time* magazine some years back, printing a portrait of Frost on the cover, placed the following beneath the picture,

ROBERT FROST
*Good fences make good neighbors*

thus implying the sentiment to be Frost's. In fact, this statement is made not by the protagonist in the poem (who might be taken to speak for Frost), but by the neighbor whose uncritical acceptance of custom the protagonist questions and whom the protagonist describes as moving ". . . in darkness as it seems to me,/Not of woods only and the shade of trees." There is no question that the phrase is a key one. It is repeated twice. But the critical blunder of not noting the dramatic context, i.e., who speaks it, leads to a total misunderstanding of the poem.

Unlikely as it may seem, it is still not uncommon to see an explication take off in strange directions, loosed by the always incredible, but never-dying belief that a poem can mean about anything the reader wants it to mean.

I am going to illustrate this by reprinting two brief explications of a poem by E. E. Cummings ("anyone lived in a pretty how town"). The first of these I believe to be a sensible explication, while the second is contradictory to it. Worse, the author of the second explication does not recognize that the two readings are contradictory; on the contrary, he specifically states that both readings are excellent and that one may see both as existing simultaneously in the poem.

## EXPLICATION I

. . . In substance it is an account of the lives of two people, "anyone" and "noone," and in theme it contrasts the response to life made by these two with the response made by the mass of people. The singularity of "anyone" and "noone" lies in their identification with a cycle of natural events rather than with routine and sterile human activities, and in their harmony with one another. Against the cyclic movement of the natural universe, described in the refrains, the poet introduces three contrapuntal elements: "anyone" and "noone," distinguished by the singular pronoun; the men and women who are also the "someones" and "everyones" as well as the "busy folk"; and the children. "Anyone" is an anonymous individual living in a particular, attractive, but carefully unspecified town who affirms the value of life by singing and dancing his responses to it. Most other people, the narrow range of whose quality is indicated by the ironic placing of "little" and "small" as if at opposite ends of the spectrum, neither know nor care for "anyone." Their lives consist of sowing negatives or denials (including the denial of love) and reaping what they have sown, finally returning to the dust from which they have come, without having achieved the joy or love which alone are capable of giving significance to life. Only a few children know that "anyone" is beloved by "noone" increasingly as time passes, and this knowledge is gradually lost to them as they grow older and begin to share the characteristics of most adults. (It seems probable that in lines 12 and 26 the poet has used "noone" not only as the

name for the woman who loves "anyone," but also in
its literal sense of "nobody," employing the pun to
make statements about the isolation of the two people
in a world full of selfish "someones.") "Anyone" and
"noone," who ironically have only a negative identity
among their human kind, are in harmony with one another and with the natural cycle; they make the appropriate (natural) responses to joy and grief; finally,
their death is not a personal division but a merging
with one another as a part of their merging with all
nature. For them death is a culmination, whereas for
the others the cycle is broken after "sleep wake hope."
They fail to see that the love and harmony achieved
by "anyone" and "noone" while alive are responsible
for a final affirmation: the joining of their bodies and
spirits to a friendly earth in which their perpetual sleep
(death) is a perpetual dream.

In the concluding stanza the statement about the
lives of most men and women, interposed between the
two refrains, stresses the eccentricity of the "everyones"
in contrast to the cycle of natural events. Centered in
themselves, limited by their denials, they move only
back and forth, reaching nothing higher than hope and
nothing more profound than sleep. Instead of the rich
completion attained by "anyone" and "noone," they are
merely cut off, while the universal and permanent "sun
moon stars rain" continue in their course.[7]

### EXPLICATION 2

. . . Cummings is telling a children's story, about
children and grown-ups and about growing-up, in
the deceptively simple-complex language of childhood.
Cummings' highly conscious and perceptive naïveté is
the mode in which he tells a fable with at least two
concurrent themes. One of these is lucidly explained
by Mr. Steinhoff and Mr. Barrows [in the preceding

explication]. . . . They read the poem as a "love-story"—and it is—of "anyone" and "noone," who saved their innocence and naturalness by avoiding the ways of the "busy folk." So it would be a lyric in praise of nonconformity.

But it is also an "unlove"-story. The fable, kindly and sweetly told to children, eases their discovery, or the reader's understanding, that "women and men" forget what children knew—how to love and be loved. And it is to this theme that stanzas 3 and 4 explicitly contribute. "anyone" and "noone" are also children (with perhaps a suggestion that "noone" is a boy's mother as he sees her). They are the ones who feel beloved and gradually forget to love. Their world contrasts with the topsy-turvy world of men and women. "anyone" and "noone" see that it is topsy-turvy and unhappy, but they grow up into it, of course ("anyone died i guess") and "forgot to remember" how it seemed and was. Love in the grown-up world is sex ("both dong and ding") and the many bells no longer float. And so "anyone" becomes, as the poem unfolds, the lost and insular self of anyone, indeed—whom no one loved anymore.

This theme of lost childhood and of lyric reconciliation has an affinity with Wordsworth ("Shades of the prison house begin to close/Upon the growing boy") but Cummings escapes the worn confines of Romantic diction by intensely and playfully exploiting the incompetent and resourceful language of children. Similar reinforcement of theme and diction may be seen in "hist whist," "(One!), the wisti-twisti barber-pole," "gee i like to think of dead," "little tree little silent Christmas tree," "my sweet old etcetera aunt lucy," "porky & porkie," and "in Just spring." In these poems and others Cummings copies or alludes to artful stammering, tongue-twisters, and boy-chants, boy-spells, and boy-swearing as a very sophisticated rhetoric that invites the reader to look sympathetically through the pseudo-innocence of the diction at familiar subjects transformed by wit, sarcasm, melancholy, tenderness, bad temper, or gaiety. Such roundabout ways into the theme of a poem often let Cummings get away with statements and invitations that would seem trite or sentimental except for the "excuse" that the childlike or childish wit affords.

If we now put together both lines of explication, the one seeing "anyone lived in a pretty how town" as a love-story, the other finding also a fable of what it costs to grow, we see that both themes develop resonantly, each with its own drama. One praises the happy and successful isolation of two lovers who keep innocence and naturalness. The other tells the "really true" story of the loss of innocence and of love that is the common lot of children growing up. And that is natural too: "sun moon stars rain." [8]

What the second explication asks one to accept is that the characters of the story are at least two different people at the same time. Or that they represent two different types at the same time. Thus the critic accepts the Barrows-Steinhoff version that "anyone" and "noone" are an adult couple who manage to live out their lives as loving individuals, who finally die, and whose creative life continues to grow in meaning through the turning of time after their death. At the same time he (the critic) says that we may also, and without any strain, see "anyone" and "noone" as children, whose "dying" is the death of childhood, and who share the common human fate of relinquishing their individuality as they grow up. (He compounds the impossibility by suggesting that "noone" may at the same time be a woman, lover of "anyone," a child of the growing-up theme which he advocates, *and* the *mother* of a boy).

As the first explication implies, the poem is cast in classic allegorical form. Just as such abstractions as Abstinence and Gluttony stand for certain kinds of human activity in older allegories, so do "anyone" and "someones" and "noone" and "everyones" create the kind of simple moral pattern of oppositional values which we have come to expect in this fictive form. These abstract, descriptive names are meant to stand for qualities which Barrows and Steinhoff, in their brief description, have for our purposes adequately suggested. These characters go through certain events which are meant to form a pattern of direct contrast. Thus the fact that "someones married their everyones" must have its direct moral contrast in some action of "anyone" and "noone," presumably "that noone loved him more by more." Now obviously, if it is to form a direct contrast with the word "married," which is meant to underline the *formal* nature of the relationship between "someones" and "everyones," the "loved" cannot be referring to the love between children. The second critic says that " 'women and men' forget what children knew—how to love and be loved." But that is not what the poem says the children knew. The children (and only a few of them at that) knew that "noone loved him." In short a few children in the "how town" were aware of this love, but they grew up and forgot about this couple.

But it is not such details with which we are concerned in this explication. Certainly had the second critic produced his theory of an " 'unlove'-story," declaring the first explication in error, then he would have been wrong, but not methodologically wrong. Many a critic has misread a work, and will again—that is part of the price one pays for committing oneself in print. But what makes this so much worse than that is this critic's insistence that two diametrically opposed readings can and do exist side by side in the same poem. He insists, in short, on a particularly egregious form of the critical position which says you can make anything you like of a poem.

The poem is an allegory. That means the poem is making, through human qualities purified and abstracted into personifications, certain simple moral distinctions. Therefore certain events take place which must be favorable or unfavorable to the characters who represent the moral attitudes the author approves. The critic cannot have it both ways. As an example, "anyone" and "noone" die. Now the second critic would have it that this can be at one and the same time their physical death after a lifetime of loving each other, and the death of their childhood, the death of this wonderful innocence and ability to love, of their becoming "someones" and "everyones." Apart from such facts as that "dong and ding" are syntactically tied to "women and men" and *contrasted* to "anyone" and "noone," apart from such facts, the critic would have us believe that we have in this death a death which is both wholly good and wholly bad (not ambiguous—all one or the other) depending on which version you choose to think about at a given moment. The fact is, everything the poet says about these deaths points to their beauty, to the continued growth of their love in death. He contrasts how they "dream their sleep" (their death is but a dream to them) with the "someones" and "everyones" who "slept their dream." (Their lives were dreams through which they slept, or they achieve no dreams in their life except the suppressed ones of sleep.) The whole series of parallelisms about anyone's and noone's deaths are a paean of praise and fulfillment, culminating in "if by yes." Now "yes" is one word Cummings never uses ironically. "Yes" *always* in his poetry stands for the creative, the outgoing, the loving individual accepting reality. This stanza is *directly* contrasted to the last stanza and to what happens in the life and death of the "everyones" and the "someones."

One is tempted to generalize and say that had the second critic been explicating his poem as part of a preparation for performance, it would have been difficult if not impossible for him to have allowed himself these conclusions. He would have had to make up his mind how he was to read the passages concerning the deaths of "anyone" and "no-one" and he would have found it quite impossible to inter-pret the event both as a pathetic failure and as an achieve-ment of lyric joy at the same instant. The oral reader must of necessity understand the dramatic situation—who is speaking, who is being spoken to, where and when the event is taking place, and what physical gestures are de-picted—and comprehend the tones that arise from that situ-ation.

The Barrows-Steinhoff explication is by no means a com-plete one, nor even accurate in all its points. Nonetheless, it does avoid the major flaws of the second. It sees the overall structure of the poem, and the details it explicates are de-veloped within that overall scheme. It is too sketchy to be a model. Too many important details are left unexplained or insufficiently developed. But it is a beginning upon which an interpreter might build a more comprehensive view of the poem.

I have spoken briefly of the kinds of literary works which usually attract explication and of several causes that often underlie misleading explications. I have spoken par-ticularly of the kind of explication which a student, and particularly an oral interpretation student, will be led to do by the nature of the occasion for which he is preparing. Robert Lowell's "Where the Rainbow Ends" affords an op-portunity to attempt such an explication on a poem with some very interesting problems.

## II

### WHERE THE RAINBOW ENDS

I saw the sky descending, black and white,
Not blue, on Boston where the winters wore
The skulls to jack-o'-lanterns on the slates,

And Hunger's skin-and-bone retrievers tore
The chickadee and shrike. The thorn tree waits          5
Its victim and tonight
The worms will eat the deadwood to the foot
Of Ararat: the scythers, Time and Death,
Helmed locusts, move upon the tree of breath;
The wild ingrafted olive and the root          10

Are withered, and a winter drifts to where
The Pepperpot, ironic rainbow, spans
Charles River and its scales of scorched-earth miles
I saw my city in the Scales, the pans
Of judgment rising and descending. Piles          15
Of dead leaves char the air—
And I am a red arrow on this graph
Of Revelations. Every dove is sold
The Chapel's sharp-shinned eagle shifts its hold
On serpent-Time, the rainbow's epitaph.          20

In Boston serpents whistle at the cold.
The victim climbs the altar steps and sings:
"Hosannah to the lion, lamb, and beast
Who fans the furnace-face of IS with wings:
I breathe the ether of my marriage feast."          25
At the high altar, gold
And a fair cloth. I kneel and the wings beat
My cheek. What can the dove of Jesus give
You now but wisdom, exile? Stand and live,
The dove has brought an olive branch to eat.[9]          30

Even a cursory reading of "Where the Rainbow Ends"
leaves strong impressions. It emanates a grim power. It is
a poem fairly thick with allusions, allusions whose precise
meaning and whose interrelationship in some cases are not
too clear. Its esthetic effect would seem to derive from complexity of sensibility rather than from delicacy of perception or tone. Despair, revulsion arise out of an apocalyptic

vision of our civilization and lead to an ambiguous conclusion in which individual salvation may be achieved only on the rebirth into a spiritual reality that is grim and bitter. But the texture of event, detail, image out of which that tone or progression of tones arises is not always clear, and weaknesses in the tonal fabric itself will remain till those questions are resolved. In short, it is not one of those poems whose clarity leaves the reader with no problems beyond a nice analysis of the precise function of each detail in the creation of the proper intonational patterns, paralingual integrations, and other aspects of a living tone. Rather, explication is necessary to achieve a primary understanding. The reader's initial difficulties are largely centered in images, local referents, and allusions which are somewhat elusive.

Before beginning a systematic review of the poem, I should like to mention several points of difficulty in it. The first is a simple difficulty that is clarified by a point of information. The "Pepperpot" is a local Boston bridge whose iron superstructure gives it this nickname. I was never sure of the meaning of this term until I heard the poet give the information in a question-and-answer period following a public reading of his poems. I had tentatively assumed it was a bridge, but couldn't tell whether the name was strictly the author's, was the legitimate name, a nickname, or had to do with its appearance or some historical association.

A more vexing difficulty is in lines 28-29:

> . . . What can the dove of Jesus give
> You now but wisdom, exile? . . .

At the present time I see no way to resolve the ambiguity that resides in the syntactical position of the word "exile." Is the poet saying, "What can the dove of Jesus give you now except wisdom and exile?" or is he addressing the "you" of the poem and saying, "What can the dove of Jesus

give you now but wisdom, O exile?" Perhaps the poet intended the ambiguity, but such an intention is of little assistance to the oral reader. For while some kinds of ambiguity can be sustained or expressed vocally, this type can
not. Each of the two meanings requires its own distinct intonational pattern.

There are other points of difficulty. Lines 2-3

> . . . where the winters wore
> The skulls to jack-o'-lanterns on the slates,

present a problem of identification. What are the skulls, the
jack-o'-lanterns, the slates? Are the skulls gargoyles on
some literal Boston roof (see "Pepperpot" for precedent)?
Are they children's school slates or blackboards? Are they
the people walking on slate sidewalks? Frankly I see no
way of being sure. None of these possibilities seem entirely
satisfactory. However, if the interpreter-explicator cannot
identify a specific image or reference, he *can* try to identify
its emotional pattern, its tone. Further, he can always look
at the poet's other poems hoping to find there the image or
reference used in a clarifying context, or at least some
more general clue to the mystery. Such a search among
Lowell's other poems does not reveal the image, but it does
suggest the following as a possible explanation of the emotional and thematic intent of the passage. Lowell, for all
he dislikes his Puritan ancestors, has a profound, and perhaps envious, admiration for those self-certain men. This
admiration would seem to be part of a larger pattern which
includes a corrosive dislike of himself and of his social contemporaries, descendants of those Puritan forefathers. This
is a pattern projected in his images again and again, and
we may have another such in this skulls-to-jack-o'-lanterns
passage. Skulls (representing somehow the harsh Puritan
sensibility of sin and death) are strong, grim, human, while
the modern jack-o'-lanterns are nothing, a child's spook, a
funny grotesque.

> . . . Every dove is sold
> The Chapel's sharp-shinned eagle shifts its hold
> On serpent-Time, the rainbow's epitaph.

This passage, lines 18-20, presents a question of reference or allusion—one suspects there is a real eagle in a real chapel. But its principal difficulty is a grammatical one. One wishes for a period after "sold," which would make two sentences of good sense. But neither of the two editions of *Lord Weary's Castle* (in which book the poem is to be found) contains any such punctuation, even though the poem was revised in two places for the second edition. Thus "sold" is apparently some sort of passive construction, with somebody trying to sell the dove something. But given the structure of line 19, that something can hardly be the eagle. Obviously any attempt to find the proper intonational patterns for these lines will be fruitless so long as the grammatical structure is unclear. Where no sense can otherwise be gained, the interpreter must risk a tentative decision, which in this case is to presume a period should occur after "sold."

The oral interpreter is left in a similar dilemma, but for different reasons, by line 21, "In Boston serpents whistle at the cold." Here the difficulty is in deciding the emotional context of the act of whistling. There is an initial vagueness as to who or what the "serpents" symbolize. Time has just previously been seen as a serpent. Are these whistling serpents the minutes or hours of the day? Are they people, seen as the evil creatures of evil times? One wonders if the act of whistling is an act of contempt for the cold or an act of amazement at the cold? These are questions which a reader might evade if he were not to read the poem aloud. I shall tentatively take them as symbols of evil whose cold natures can whistle contemptuously at mere physical cold.

The title introduces the poem's basic comparison of the

speaker's plight in the modern world with the Noah story. At the end of the flood, God sent Noah a rainbow as "a token of a covenant" that "neither shall all flesh be cut off any more by the waters of the flood; neither shall there any more be a flood to destroy the earth" (Genesis 9). Less forcefully, the old fairy tale about the pot of gold at the end of the rainbow is called to mind as another thread in the pattern of elusive hopes.

"And Jehovah saw that the wickedness of man was great in the earth, and that every imagination of the thoughts of his heart was only evil continually" (Genesis 6.5). This is how Jehovah saw the world before the flood, and it is how the speaker in the poem sees his contemporary world. The poem is about that speaker's world, i.e., not necessarily the real world, but the world as it really is to him. The poem's despair is both personal and societal. It starts with "I saw," and the resolution of the vision of earthly hell, whose images are the corrosive ones of industrial blight, is a personal one.

The first stanza (let us ignore the already mentioned difficulty with the third line) develops the basic comparison between the Noah-flood story and the speaker in the modern industrial state. Dramatically speaking, in the first stanza the speaker sees the onset of the flood, the "sky descending." It is a descent appropriately Puritan, "black and white,/Not blue," and we take it that the speaker's historic Boston culture is for him a winter in which the abstractions Hunger and Time and Death work their destructive will on the gentle (the chickadee) as well as the brutal (the shrike). The speaker in this apocalyptic vision sees himself in a role that has affinities not only to Noah but also to Jesus ("The thorn tree waits/Its victim"). Indeed, the central dramatic movement of the poem is a shift from one life to another, a rebirth, the losing of one's life to gain life. But no perfect world lies beyond that rebirth. Noah's descendants certainly forgot nothing of the evil of the pre-flood world. The worm rides in the very keel of the ark just as the crucifixion left a world which organizes its evil on an ever vaster and more apocalyptic scale. Indeed, the end of an epoch is implied not only in the Noah allusion and in the later allusions to Revelations, but also in the reference to Paul's letter to the Romans (ii.17) where he discusses the grafting of the gentiles to the Judaic root. One may speculate that the end is a personal one, perhaps primarily so.

"Ironic" is the second direct pun, the first was "deadwood." Both have their similarities in that they refer to a structure, its material. ("Deadwood" signifies both the strong, heavy timbers placed horizontally along the bow and stern of a boat and the dead branches on a tree.) The reference to the ark insists on one side of the pun, the references to tree and olive insist on the other. Thus, the author causes the word to make its own moral comment on itself. The deadwood is an essential part of the ark. At the same time it is deadwood in the other sense and carries in the heart of the ship the worms of decay across the cleansing flood. Similarly the bridge is iron, but in its rainbow shape it is ironic. It does not lead to the pot of gold. It leads to an iron land, a hard, scaly (serpenty?) land. "Scales" in itself is another pun. When first used, it carries both the meaning just mentioned and the notion of scales of miles as on a map. (We must assume, it seems clear, some kind of stop—a period, preferably—after the word "miles.") Then, when used a second time, the word is capitalized into an abstraction and becomes part of the next personification, that of judgment weighing the city. The judgment is rendered not in terms of a flood of water but of fire. It is a burned-out land, where some remnants of smoke still "char the air." The speaker, too, becomes an abstraction, a simple flesh and blood device for pointing out these images of desolation.

Here the nadir is reached. Unlike Noah, the speaker has

no doves. All, in this commercial world, are "sold." Is this a pun? Sold out, as well as simply, straightforwardly sold? If the eagle is the U.S. symbol, then the state and its religion are confined to the mastery of worldly power—the end of the rainbow's hope. There is no help and no dove to send for help.

A remarkable shift in perspective occurs at this stanza break. Up to now, the speaker has referred to himself in the first person, "I saw," "I saw," "I am." Now, as if the saving death that will restore life has come upon him, he sees himself in the third person. *He* is now the victim the thorn tree was awaiting in the first stanza. He climbs the altar a "victim," a sacrifice, if you will. "Lion," "lamb," and "beast" are words which appear in different contexts throughout the Bible, but this reference is probably to Revelations 5 and 6 which describe the opening of the seven seals: "And I saw a strong angel proclaiming with a great voice, Who is worthy to open the book, and to loose the seals thereof? . . . behold the Lion that is of the tribe of Judah, the root of David, hath overcome to open the book and the seven seals thereof. And I saw . . . a Lamb standing. . . ." As each seal is broken, a different beast symbolizes what is revealed. Thus, the lion, lamb, and beast are various aspects of God, the source which creates the future by fanning that which is to burning heat. "IS" may also be seen as another aspect of God. The victim praises the God to whom he is an offering; the mighty power which creates all that is, that spoke to Moses out of the burning bush commanding him to lead his people out of bondage (Exodus 3.1-12), identifying himself as "I AM THAT I AM: and he said, Thus shalt thou say unto the children of Israel, I AM hath sent me unto you" (Exodus 3.13-14). The images of death and rebirth are held ambiguously here, with "ether" and "marriage feast," two powerful opposing concepts, forcibly conjoined. The wings fan

IS—all physical reality—and the wings therefore fan the speaker who cannot escape his mortality.

And here is where the oral reader must decide on the meaning of ". . . wisdom, exile." Two poems lie there. In the one case the conclusion would see the speaker moving into exile—what can the dove of Jesus bring you but wisdom and exile; you must live with the bitter peace of spiritual apartness. In the second case the poem's conclusion would assume the speaker to have been an exile and to be now moving into a greater wisdom, a return to life on a wiser level. In this interpretation the bitter "death" of the marriage feast leads to a new reconciliation in which the speaker can no longer live in the luxury of apartness from the hell around him. He can no longer be simply an arrow pointing out the world's evil. The Old Testament stance of the prophet who stands apart and damns is at an end, and the speaker must "stand and live," accepting his mortal involvement.

Obviously these two interpretations are far from each other. A person who would read the poem aloud cannot ride both horses, for he is under the necessity of creating these abstractions into a living attitude. Whichever he decides is right (and I may say that I prefer the second direction), the ending itself is a grim business. For the uncured olive is bitter, and in any case it is not the fruit that must be eaten, but the whole branch. There *is* a dove as yet unsold despite the speaker's earlier denial, but the gift it brings is not the end of crime and evil, any more than in Noah's story. It brings simply the reality of life, the bitter knowledge of one's own mortal involvement in all mortality, as Noah himself, good man though he was, was the seed of the misery that followed.

I have several times mentioned that the tone of the speaker's voice is prophetic. Indeed, in that sense it is a traditional voice and has its definite relationship to the

Prophetic Voice we hear in the Bible and in later secular works. It is a voice which is at once personal and objective. Its world is bodied forth with the heat of a personal vision. Yet, to be convincing, we must sense an objectivity—a self-lessness, if you will—about the evidence which is marshalled to describe that world. For as a lover's voice describes and praises at the same instant, the prophet's voice describes and denounces in the same figure. (Is the prophet the lover who loves too well, who expects more of truth and beauty than the object of his attention can fulfill?) Lowell's technique in this poem is constantly to skirt the edges of pure vision, convincing us of the *reality* of the vision by tying it to accurate, realistic detail. The brutality of New England winter is the first such realistic detail. Indeed the sky does seem more black and white than blue. Indeed hunger does then stalk the kingdom of living creatures human and nonhuman. (The opening of each stanza reiterates this symbol of fierce if aimless winter.)

But the winter soon is being described through that most moralistic of figures, the allegorical personification, Hunger, and then only a phrase intervenes before we come upon half a stanza of pure symbolic vision in the manner of Revelations.

The second stanza, however, never quite leaves the real scene, for its purpose, through realistic local scenic details and through language connected with commerce (scales, graph), is to convince us of the truth of the judgment of the urban earth. But the first line of the last stanza moves away from the real winter to a climactic summation of the spiritual winter. This line is immediately followed by a shift. I have already pointed to the fact that this is a shift in person —a shift from the protagonist's speaking of himself in the first person to speaking of himself in the third.

This shift is notable in other ways. Up to this point the protagonist's eyes have been on two kinds of scenes, a broad sweep of devastated landscape and freezing sky or a purely imaginary vision of the wide world ("The thorn tree waits . . ."). Now, in the last stanza, the protagonist moves indoors, the scope is delimited, private, intense in a different way. Here at the altar is the center of everything. The scorched earth, now frozen, the IS, the material world, is excited to flame—to life—by the wings of the deity. The same wings fan the red cheeks of the protagonist. The wide waste, which he earlier surveyed, and the inner waste become one in the bitter marriage of the protagonist to God, and through God to the world. Thus, granted the second meaning to the poem, the prophet's voice moves away from its traditional tone at the end. The note of condemnation, of lashing out, becomes paradoxically more personal as the protagonist finds himself a part of the wide waste.

Finally, in an olive (such as the dove brought to Noah), the meaning of God's covenant, both in the rainbow and in the crucified victim promising redemption, becomes plain. It is not a covenant to end anything, but a constant beginning which is harsh and unsentimental. There is no escape. The price is to "stand and live." (This last line and a half appears on the poet's father's tombstone, and it is interesting to speculate on the meaning of this command in the light of the poet's later autobiographical writing concerning the failure of his father's life.)

There is, as we said at the beginning, a feeling of grim power in the poem. No doubt this feeling arises mostly from the nature of the images, Biblical allusions, and the theme of the poem. But I think it is much enhanced by three musical and prosodic elements. First, the poem is rigidly syllabic metrically, and within that syllabic meter there is a very heavy iambic rhythm, given variety by pause and by certain rhythmic variations, the most prominent being xxx/. Second, this sense of regular rhythm is converted into a powerful rhythm by the relatively heavy use of consonantal echoes and repetitions as compared to the assonantal echoes. And third, the rigid line and powerful beat are both heavily modified by the particular use of enjambment, or run-on lines. The line ends are firmly marked by true rhyme (very firmly—all but two terminal rhyming words of the thirty are monosyllables), but the rigidity of the syllabic line and the marching rhythm are given an ongoing rush marked by abrupt and unexpected stops through the device of continuous run-on lines and long sentences which are likely to break or end in unorthodox places ("Of judgment rising and descending. Piles/ . . .").

These, then, are the challenges of this poem for the oral reader: a series of difficult decisions relating to the meaning of the poem; a tortured, nightmarish vision of the world, to be dealt with honestly but without melodrama; a music which is like the denotative and connotative matter, powerful and complex, but not particularly fine-drawn or subtle.

Explication is an attempt to see as a whole the poem whose parts are not only in harmony (a rather static word) but actively operating to illuminate and to delimit the experience encompassed in the entire poem. Explication tries to do this, as much as is possible, out of the common cultural experience which the reader and the author share. Who is speaking? Who is being spoken to? Under what conditions, in what surroundings, is the action evolving? What are the kind, weight, associations of the words? These are the explicator's first concerns.

Naturally no work of art exists in a vacuum and therefore no work of art is completely to be understood as it stands in splendid isolation, as my resorting to Lowell's other works and to the Bible demonstrate. The oral interpreter is especially aware of the work of art as a work of communication, a work whose intonations are real, whose farthest phrase will alter slightly in tone at the modification of the tone of any part. His explication, then, should properly lead to an interpretation—that is, to the same sort of living, creative commitment to meaning which occurs when an instrumentalist plays a great score.

Fortunately, I was able to query the author directly concerning some of the more difficult points raised in the explication above. The answers to my questions arrived *after* I had written the above, and since I wished to preserve as much as possible the intrinsic nature of my view of the poem, I did not think it proper to rewrite the essay in order to incorporate what I had learned from the author. However, I think his comments are of special interest and I should like to reproduce them here, followed by some random thoughts that Lowell's elucidations raise for explications in general and mine in particular:

1) The slates are old-fashioned slate gravestones, the skulls the conventional death's heads on them, and they become jack-o'-lanterns through the kindly attrition of wind and weather, and perhaps the decay in a belief in the Christian horrors of death.

2) The Chapel is King's Chapel, a wrenlike 18th century building near the Boston State House. There's an eagle on the lectern. The eagle stands for the fixed force of the old dogma, time is the human, changing and relative, what is always, perhaps vainly trying to escape from Law. The Dove is a reference to Christ and the money-lenders, also the Holy Spirit. I am contrasting the Church law and the experience of grace. There should be a comma or a period after "sold," Alas.

3) The serpents whistling at the cold is an intentionally grotesque image, meaning whistling in the dark, vain bluster, and this is combined with the almost opposed meaning of cold blooded creatures being by

nature able to defy cold. The serpents are evil defying the tortures of man and god, and nature rather jauntily being able to stand up to the harsh climate.

4) The exile is entirely the you of the poem. There's no ambiguity, unless it's that the word exile almost cancels the possibility of wisdom. Things are so hopeless that only the miraculous everything can now be given.[10]

I missed the possibility of the slates being headstones, though I did see it as probably a local reference. In fact, one of the things that impresses the explicator about this poem is how firmly it is tied to a local habitation, and how apparently unconscious the poet is that someone outside Boston (and most of the world is, even if Boston is the hub) might not be aware of these details. Skulls as a frequent motif for headstones is, I suspect, a New England Puritan phenomenon; I cannot remember having observed it elsewhere. It is especially instructive to see that it was possible, despite not knowing the specific image, to extrapolate from other evidence the general emotional, thematic purpose and pattern of the passage. The knowledge of the Chapel as a specific referent is invaluable, but must be relatively unknown to other than native Bostonians.

Apparently my question concerning the ambiguity involved in the word "exile" must have been unclear. The ambiguity is not one of person, but rather one of time. There is no question that the person is the "you" of the poem. The question, rather, is whether the dove is bringing wisdom to one already exiled, or bringing wisdom and exile simultaneously. However, Lowell's further comments are interesting in that they do not resolve the ambiguous possibilities of the last lines.

The "serpents whistling" line would seem, as Lowell suggests and as I intuited, to contain two diametrically opposed emotions. I think the oral interpreter will find himself under the necessity to resolve this ambiguity, for I don't believe they are compatible so long as one entertains the common notion of a blusterer as one who cannot really perform up to his talk. In this sense, the serpents cannot both bluster against the cold (pretend a power to withstand it which they do not have) and at the same time actually have the power. Thus the interpreter must, I think, see these serpents as defiers who can deliver on their defiance. I do not know how one could read this passage so as to convey simultaneously "vain bluster," and "jauntily being able to stand up to the harsh climate."

## NOTES

1. Simone Weil, *The Iliad; or, The Poem of Force,* trans. Mary McCarthy (Wallingford, Penna.: Pendle Hill, 1956); first appeared in this country in the November 1945 issue of *Politics.*

2. Ernest Jones, *Hamlet and Oedipus* (London: V. Gollancz, 1949); a revision of an essay first published in 1910.

3. Royal Ms. App. 58, fol. $5^a$.

4. Richard R. Griffith, "Westron Wynde When Wyll Thow blowe," *Explicator,* XXI (May 1963), #69.

5. From *Collected Poems of Edwin Arlington Robinson* (New York: The Macmillan Co., 1940), p. 346.

6. From *Complete Poems of Robert Frost* (New York: Henry Holt, 1949), p. 270.

7. Herbert C. Barrows, Jr., and William R. Steinhoff, "Cummings' ANYONE LIVED IN A PRETTY HOW TOWN," *Explicator,* IX (Oct. 1950), #1.

8. Arthur Carr, "Cummings' ANYONE LIVED IN A PRETTY HOW TOWN," *Explicator,* XI (Nov. 1952), #6.

9. From *Lord Weary's Castle* (New York: Harcourt, Brace, 1946), p. 69.

10. From a response, dated April 21, 1965, to certain questions I addressed to Mr. Lowell. Used with his permission.

RECOMMENDED READING

In order to understand the important place of explication in literary studies today, it is necessary to realize that it has operated generally on two levels. Both of these levels, the professional criticism and the textbook, have perhaps their most important roots in I. A. Richards' *Practical Criticism* (London: K. Paul, Trench, Trubner, 1929). The contribution of both poets and scholars to the New Criticism (the literary movement largely responsible for increased attention to explication) has been considerable. Here are some of the significant early scholarly or theoretical volumes in this movement:

R. P. Blackmur, *The Double Agent: Essays in Craft and Elucidation* (New York: Arrow Editions, 1935).

Cleanth Brooks, *Modern Poetry and the Tradition* (Chapel Hill: University of North Carolina Press, 1939).

Kenneth Burke, *Counter-Statement* (New York: Harcourt, Brace, 1931). *The Philosophy of Literary Form* (Baton Rouge: Louisiana State University Press, 1941).

William Empson, *Seven Types of Ambiguity* (London: Chatto and Windus, 1930); revised ed. (New York: New Directions, 1947).

F. R. Leavis, *Revaluation: Tradition and Development in English Poetry* (London: Chatto and Windus, 1936).

John Crowe Ransom, *The World's Body* (New York: Charles Scribner's Sons, 1938). *The New Criticism* (Norfolk, Conn.: New Directions, 1941).

Allen Tate, *Reactionary Essays on Poetry and Ideas* (New York: Charles Scribner's Sons, 1936).

Austin Warren, *Rage for Order: Essays in Criticism* (Chicago: University of Chicago Press, 1948).

Edmund Wilson, *Axel's Castle: A Study in the Imaginative Literature of 1870–1930* (New York: Charles Scribner's Sons, 1931).

Yvor Winters, *Primitivism and Decadence: A Study of American Experimental Poetry* (New York: Arrow Editions, 1937).

Elizabeth Drew's *Discovering Poetry* (New York: W. W. Norton, 1933) is an example of several early books which sought to use the techniques of the New Criticism to open a wider audience to poetry, especially modern poetry. These books culminated in *Understanding Poetry*, a textbook by Cleanth Brooks and Robert Penn Warren (New York: Henry Holt, 1938); 3rd ed. (New York: Holt, Rinehart, and Winston, 1960). I think it is fair to say that this book revolutionized introductory courses in poetry and naturally led to a host of books developing analytic and explicative techniques for the classroom.

Here are a few later scholarly or theoretical books which should be of interest to the explicator:

Joseph Warren Beach, *Obsessive Images: Symbolism in Poetry of the 1930s and 1940s,* ed. William Van O'Connor (Minneapolis: University of Minnesota Press, 1960).

Reuben Brower, *The Fields of Light: An Experiment in Critical Reading* (New York: Oxford University Press, 1951).

Donald Davie, *Purity of Diction in English Verse* (London: Chatto and Windus, 1952).

Elizabeth Drew, *Poetry: A Modern Guide to Its Understanding and Enjoyment* (New York: W. W. Norton, 1959).

William Empson, *The Structure of Complex Words* (New York: New Directions, 1951).

John Wain, ed., *Interpretations: Essays on Twelve English Poems* (London: Routledge and K. Paul, 1955).

For the student interested in finding explications of a given author or in studying explication as a form of criticism, there are two sources which are indispensable. The magazine entiled *The Explicator* (Box 10, University of South Carolina, Columbia, So. Carolina) is devoted entirely to queries and explications. The explications are seldom very long, are usually in the nature of a brief development of an insight toward a work or part of a work. The magazine began in 1942. *Very important* is the *Check-List of Explication* which has appeared annually in *The Explicator* since 1946. The check list is actually an annual bibliography of books and articles which are in some way related to explication. The other important source is a book compiled by George Arms and Joseph M. Kuntz entitled *Poetry Explication*. This book was first published in 1950 and covered explications between the years 1925–1949. However, a revised edition was published by Alan Swallow, Denver, in 1962, covering explications published during the years 1950–1959. This book, besides containing a useful bibliography, is arranged by author and then further subdivided into individual works. It is, therefore, quite simple to find all the explications on a given poem of which these editors are aware.

## Projects

The only exercise which is very valuable in learning the explicative method is to write explications. The following projects may be used as the bases for short papers analyzing selections to be read aloud in class.

1. Look up a poem with several explications by different critics in Arms and Kuntz *Poetry Explication* (described above) and try writing a brief explication of your own, then read what the critics said and see what you or they

missed. At the end of your paper, append a brief discussion in which you compare the professional explications, if possible analyzing what each was trying to achieve, and point out the comparative success or failure of each, including your own.

2. A similar project could be constructed utilizing any one of various collections of critical essays on a single author. For instance, there is Prentice-Hall's *Twentieth Century Views* series, which includes collections of essays on such authors as Eliot and Frost. A book such as the one on Robert Frost (edited by James Cox) contains many fascinating and conflicting explications and partial explications against which to test your own understanding.

3. Several good exercises in explication can be constructed utilizing *The Case for Poetry* by Frederick L. Gwynn, Ralph W. Condee, and Arthur O. Lewis, Jr., 2nd ed. (Englewood Cliffs: Prentice-Hall, 1965). This book is a critical anthology, and following certain of the poems conflicting explications can be found. A good place for the oral interpreter to begin might be with those explications that clearly conflict on the poem's tone. For example:

    a. Read Blake's "The Tyger" and the "case" which follows (pp. 25-27). Write a brief discussion in which you describe the tone as set forth in explications A, B, and C, and evaluate the explications. Be prepared to read the poem aloud in class, demonstrating each of the three tones.

    b. Read Eliot's "Sweeney Among the Nightingales" and the "critique" and "case" which follow (pp. 112-115). From among the conflicting points of view, either select one or develop your own, and write an explication of the poem. At the end of your explication, discuss how A and B of the "case" might lead to different oral interpretations.

    c. Read Hardy's "The Darkling Thrush" and the

"case" which follows (pp. 145-147). Write a defense of A, B, or C of the "case" and refute the positions taken in the two you reject (i.e., if you defend A, then refute B and C).

4. Anthony Ostroff, ed., *The Contemporary Poet as Artist and Critic* (Boston: Little, Brown, 1964) publishes three explications each (all by poets) of eight different poems; in each case the poet himself evaluates the explications. Many valuable lessons are to be learned from the Ostroff book, including the fact that there is no final, definitive explication possible, only explications offering degrees and kinds of illumination (some of these explications also make clear how an attempt at explication can reveal more concerning the explicator than it does concerning the poem). In light of these statements, discuss any one of the eight sections in Ostroff's book. From what point of view does each explicator seem to see the poem? What are the apparent advantages and limitations of this point of view?

5. Any of the projects suggested above for poems may be constructed for fiction explications: e.g., find conflicting explications and write an evaluative discussion of them. (I have suggested that you concern yourself primarily with poems because they have been the subject of major explicative effort in our time.) Explications of stories and novels also appear in *The Explicator* and in the new journal *Studies in Short Fiction*. Invaluable aids in locating various explications of short fiction are Jarvis Thurston, et al., *Short Fiction Criticism* . . . (Denver: Alan Swallow, 1960) and Warren S. Walker, *Twentieth Century Short Story Explication* . . . (Hampton, Conn.: Shoe String Press, 1961).

# CHAPTER TWO

# FORMAL ANALYSIS:

## Long Day's Journey into Night
## as Aesthetic Object

### CHESTER CLAYTON LONG

*At the time when he is constructing his Plots, and engaged on the Diction in which they are worked out, the poet should remember (1) to put the actual scenes so far as possible before his eyes. In this way, seeing everything with the vividness of an eye-witness as it were, he will devise what is appropriate, and be least likely to overlook incongruities. . . . (2) As far as may be, too, the poet should even act his story with the very gestures of his personages. Given the same natural qualifications, he who feels the emotions to be described will be the most convincing; distress and anger, for instance, are portrayed most truthfully by one who is feeling them at the moment. Hence it is that poetry demands a man with a special gift for it, or else one with a touch of madness in him; the former can easily assume the required mood, and the latter may be actually beside himself with emotion (Aristotle, The Poetics, Chap. 17).*

*There remains plot* (mythos), *and concerning this there has been an extraordinary amount of confusion among commentators on the* Poetics. . . . *In both senses plot is clearly something the poet constructs, the difference being that, whereas in the second[ary] sense plot is conceived of as a part or substrate* (*though the most important one*) *of tragic form, in the first* [primary] *sense it is the tragic form itself in its completest actuality* (R. S. Crane, The Languages of Criticism and the Structure of Poetry).

# I

If a man wants to see a whole image of life, one place he can find it is in a dramatic, narrative, or lyric image of life. For these poetic objects have a completeness built into them that life often appears to lack when it is perceived from a day-to-day point of view.

Consequently, one of the pleasures we experience in literature can be related to literature's ability to give its image of life a formal completeness. This formal completeness is a function that operates in literature in combination with its more obvious life-imaging function. While the two elements, life images and formal completeness, are never actually separate in literature, they can, for the purposes of study, be distinguished from one another. In a practical sense, perhaps this element of formal completeness is one of the things we refer to when we say of some pieces of literature that they give us a feeling of wholeness. In this chapter we will be specifically concerned with applying a method of analysis which will supply us with some concrete words for explaining clearly to others what causes part of this feeling of wholeness that literature arouses in us.

It is reported that Chinese court officials, during the age of the great empires of China, carried objects made of jade in their hands. The jade objects apparently served no useful function in the ordinary sense of that word. They were apparently beautifully formed and carved with no other known purpose than that of being carried in the hand.

As the courtier walked through the complicated and probably hectic day at court, fulfilling his tasks, he was no doubt assailed by the ordinary complexities and frustrations that face us in our own everyday life. There were probably agreements waiting to be completed between groups of people, which could not be fulfilled immediately. There was probably suspense caused by only partially completing numerous errands and other business. The courtier probably had to wait quite often for final settlement in regard to social engagements, court favors, and the like. These business tasks and items of courtly procedure and ceremony were no doubt performed as punctually as possible in order that (1) the courtier could maintain his grasp on the position he had previously arrived at in the affairs of the Emperor's court, or that (2) the courtier could acquire further favor and influence necessary to his advancement (which would probably lead indirectly to an increase in his monetary wealth and land holdings). The court activity, then, was primarily *acquisitive* in nature.

But what of the jade handpiece? Shaped to fit his hand alone, it must have served as an outlet for some other drive beyond its value as an acquired symbol of status. Could we not suppose that as the courtier went through the business of the day, confronted often with disappointment and the frustration of not being able to complete much of his court business, his fingertips tracing the delicately perfect design and form of the jade object satisfied his need to find completeness and order in the world outside himself? The handpiece, then, in its completeness as an object, must have enabled the courtier to be *tangibly* aware of order and design in the world external to his own physical and psychological being. It must have stood as a reassuring reference to completed order and design in the external world.

Man has, since the beginning of recorded time, constantly valued objects which have had no other purpose than to be complete and ordered within themselves. The jade hand-piece is only one example of many such objects.

Beauty is that, we may suppose, which man finds at any given moment to be sufficient to itself: a stone, a poem, the sculptured contours of a racing car. Beauty occasions what appears to be a moment of perception detached from desire or action, wherein the senses of sight, touch, taste, hearing, and movement are extended into the pattern of the object which is being perceived. The perception of beauty, then, involves *contemplation,* not *acquisition.*

But notice that in the case of the racing car, both our conscious perceptive drives, *acquisitive* and *contemplative,* are appealed to simultaneously. The racing car goes fast, and we desire to acquire, or take possession of, this instrument of speed and power. We desire to make it instrumental in some practical activity, such as getting from one place to another faster, or in satisfying our desire to manipulate it with our physical being. However, at the same time, the beauty of its design (functional or not) has no actual acquisitive value. We cannot manipulate the racing car's beauty in any physical sense. We can only perceive it, *know* that its beauty exists. Yet one of the primary motivations we have for wishing to possess it is to enable us continually to perceive and experience its special, nonacquisitive value, its beauty.

To put it in another way, we can say that the racing car's beauty has its own special kind of usefulness, its own special capacity to please, though its beauty cannot be actually manipulated, used, or consumed in any practical or instrumental way. The beauty of the racing car's contours is useful because that beauty provides an outlet for our contemplative drives, which are as evident as our acquisitive drives. The racing car's beauty has the capacity to please us because the experiencing of this outlet gives us great pleasure.

Some literary works, stories, lyrics, essays, as well as plays, have the dual qualities of the racing car. They have a message we can instrumentalize or make practical use of, or more simply, acquire, as we can acquire and make practical use of the racing car's speed and power. Clifford Odets' play *Waiting for Lefty* is a clear example of this kind of literary work. It is obvious when we watch this play that we are supposed to get the message that the capitalist is crushing the laborer, that this is wrong, and that we are expected to do something about it in order to improve society. This is of course the only kind of poem Plato would have allowed in his Republic—and, we hear, the only kind of play Mr. Khrushchev favored in his Republics when he was in power. But *Waiting for Lefty,* in addition to its acquirable message content, also has a formal beauty (as the beautiful contours of the racing car's body have a formal beauty), which we can contemplate or extend our contemplative faculties and drives into.

The study of *form* is a study of the *relationships* that exist between *all* the individual elements in any single piece of literature. It is not primarily a study of the specific nature of any particular element in literature, such as imagery, meaning, structure, action, language, or style. The study of form treats the piece of literature as a unique and whole object. It does this first through observing particular relationships between elements in the piece and finally through attempting to induct and synthesize a general description of how the piece relates all of its structures of elements into a unique whole.

In this way, formal analysis provides an organic picture of the unique wholeness of the piece. In doing this it provides a context of perception in which (1) any specific element can be perceived in its relationship within the piece to any other specific element, and (2) one or more specific elements may be perceived in the light of their relationship to the whole.

Formal analysis, then, provides a clear image of the overall *means* through which individual elements in a piece of literature relate themselves into larger structures; and it provides a clear image of the *manner* in which the larger structural elements, such as narrative, description, scene, dialogue, character, sequences of events, acts, chapters, books, relate themselves into a concrete whole. This end product of inductive formal analysis, the *formal description,* provides, in effect, an image of the unifying power of the piece, which can be referred to technically as its *dynamis,* or working power, of which the central controlling principle is its *form.*

This mode of perceiving literature is clearly related to our previous remarks concerning the mode of the perception of beauty. For when we train ourselves to perceive the form of a piece of literature, we are indulging in a contemplative mode of behavior, not in an acquisitive one. As the perception of *beauty occasions what appears to be a moment of perception detached from desire or action, wherein the senses of sight, touch, taste, hearing, and movement are extended into the pattern of the object which is being perceived,* so does the perception of form.

Therefore, this essay about Eugene O'Neill's play *Long Day's Journey into Night\** will concentrate on the nonacquirable, or contemplative, aspects of the play, its formal beauty. This essay will not, however, ignore the play's acquirable message content, for that is a part of its form. Let us then begin to discover those aspects of the play that appeal to our contemplative drives, the play's formal aspects.

\* New Haven: Yale University Press, 1956. All page numbers cited by quotations from the play refer to this edition.

# II

Eugene O'Neill was never thoroughly happy with any of the productions of his plays. Directors frequently wanted to cut them, and actors were generally mystified as to how they could deliver a dialogue style that was like nothing they had ever encountered in their previous acting experience. This is not strange, however, when we consider that O'Neill was constantly experimenting with dramatic form. The directors' and the actors' experience and training simply had not prepared them to cope with the forms O'Neill constantly presented them with. Tradition is a hard thing for the creative artist to surmount in the theater.

It is only natural, then, that every director and actor who has approached this play has attempted to overcome what he sees as one of its most obvious difficulties: not much *happens* in the play, in the ordinary sense of that word. Productions tend to cut the dialogue or to quicken the pace of the scenes with much physical movement. But perhaps this is not a play of *action* or even essentially a play of *conflict*. Rather than begin our study of the play by classifying it in relation to other plays, let us set out only with the notion that the play may possibly be unique. Keeping this possibility in mind, we can proceed to discover what is unique about the play's form. Having discovered the uniqueness of the play's form, we can proceed to discover something about the play's emotional impact on an audience. For "talky" or not, when this play is on the stage, or when the scenes are read aloud, it has the capacity to stun its hearers and, perhaps even more important, to deeply move those who perform it.

Most dramatic theorists in the past have concluded that the center of dramatic power must reside either in *action* or *conflict*. They have appended all sorts of stipulative systems to the design of these two aspects of dramatic content that attempt to explain why certain plays are successful.

The action creates suspense, which is resolved by a climactic event and finished off with a denouement or explanation of unresolved minor and major aspects of the action. Or the conflict is made meaningful by its progressive development and clear issue in favor of one or another of the principal characters or in some cases left unresolved in a state of maximum tension as the play ends (and most of these latter explanations have to do with works in the modern or contemporary periods of dramatic writing). Let us observe what happens if we try to analyze the principle of this play's structure as consisting either of action or of conflict. We'll begin to understand why theatrical producers who are confined by these two categories are bewildered by this play.

It begins just after breakfast and ends just after midnight of the same twenty-four-hour period. During that brief span of time, only two things "occur" *in the present time* of the play that are of great consequence. Mary Tyrone becomes readdicted to morphine, and Edmund Tyrone is diagnosed as tubercular. In a sense, both of these things are pretty much suspected to be true anyway by the majority of the characters, so that their revelation does not come as much of a surprise to the characters or to us. What does rather shock some of the characters, and incidentally us, the audience, is the way in which the other family members react to this information. They spend more time talking about the remote past than they do about the immediate present. As a matter of fact, the most poignant scene in the play is the reënactment by the mother of her having left a convent many years before in order to marry James Tyrone, Sr., the father in the play.

The play also seems to be one long series of family quarrels. The intensity of the quarrels grows progressively more violent and hateful as the ordinary hours of the day progress from breakfast, through lunch and dinner, and ends only when it is time for the family to go to bed. But when we try to explain the power of the play in terms of its conflict in the family quarrels, we are again at a loss. For the quarrels in the play never seem to be resolved: they have no issue, they are continuous and nothing seems to be solved by them. As a matter of fact, the final quarrel in the play is simply interrupted by the ghostly appearance of the mother, shortly after midnight, trailing her wedding dress behind her, grotesquely intoxicated with morphine, and talking not of her present horrifying situation but of the moment when she left the convent. The sight of her causes the drunken father and brothers simply to turn and listen to her, while they unceremoniously drop the quarrel they had been having, letting all its issues (one of them concerning the mother's health) hang in midair. With the mother's final speech, the play ends. Nothing is resolved, nor, for that matter, are any of the issues of the quarrels ever succinctly and clearly stated, for the characters are quite drunk (or in the case of the mother, under the influence of morphine) for the great majority of the play's time.

In any ordinary terms, then, action, conflict, or what have you, does not seem to be the central principle which makes the play work, hang together, or hold an audience spellbound for two hours in the theater. Since it does work so successfully, however, there must be something about the play that makes it possible for it to do so.

Certainly this play leaves all its issues up in the air. This is true even of the major issues in the play: Mary's morphine addiction and Edmund's tuberculosis. But though the issues of the play's conflicts or action seem not to be resolved and are left hanging, Mary's final speech does seem to appropriately end the play for us. Mary's final speech does not solve any conflicts (it seems rather to complicate them). It certainly does not complete any major set of events, tying them all together, and yet Mary's final speech seems to be a climax of some sort. *How shall we explain the peculiar power of this dramatic work?* Well, it is possible that some other aspect of dramatic structure or content makes this play work, even though the two most used concepts of what a drama is do not. Let us then make a list of aspects of dramatic writing, keeping in mind that we are referring to these items in the most general conditions for drama: actors speaking to one another on a stage.

| | | |
|---|---|---|
| Plot | Form | Fourth wall |
| Character | Imitation | Arena |
| Scene | Surrealism | Proscenium |
| Dialogue | Naturalism | Stage |
| Setting | Expressionism | Empathy |
| Thought | Agent | Act |
| Emotion | Action | Period |
| Passion | Discovery | Rhythm |
| Fantasy | Motivation | Verse |
| Event | Entrance | Prose |
| Complication | Exit | Tragedy |
| Suspense | Decor | Comedy |
| Conflict | Stage effect | Gesture |
| Irony | Mood | Revelation |
| Meaning | Tension | Reversal |
| Content | Catharsis | |
| Structure | Aesthetic distance | |

The list could go on for quite some time. All of us could probably add to the list and should feel free to do so as our analysis continues.

Now, with this list of aspects of the drama in mind, let's construct a more or less step-by-step, more or less reportorial brief of what is going on in the play, keeping our terms in mind, and after that seeing if any one or any combination of these aspects seems to epitomize the dramatic activity.

## ACT I

This act takes place at about 8:30 A.M. of a day in August 1912. The family has just finished breakfast. The mother, Mary, and the father, James Tyrone, Sr., enter the stage living room from the dining room, where the two boys, Edmund and James, Jr., are laughing and talking after breakfast. Mary chides Tyrone about his real-estate speculating, worries about Edmund's "summer cold." Tyrone nags her about being careful not to get so distraught that she succumbs again to her own "illness." Mary asks not to be "watched" so constantly. The boys have been laughing and joking offstage during this conversation between the parents, and Tyrone guesses they are scheming to get some of his money.

Edmund and James, Jr., enter and jest with their father, who takes it sourly and begins to lecture them. But the mother steers them away from the quarrel. The conversation turns back to the joke the brothers had been sharing at breakfast. Edmund tells the joke, which has to do with Shaughnessy, one of Tyrone's tenants who rents a small farm bordering the estate of Harker, a Standard Oil millionaire. Harker had come to Shaughnessy's place and complained of Shaughnessy's pigs having used his ice pond for a wallow. Whereupon Shaughnessy had ridiculously accused Harker of having tried to poison Shaughnessy's pigs. But Tyrone, though obviously amused, perversely attacks his sons again about their laziness, lack of manners, socialism, and so forth. Tyrone's attack so upsets Edmund (who appears to be quite ill), that Edmund leaves. James, Jr., turns on Tyrone angrily for this, saying that Edmund is quite ill, but Tyrone is unsuccessful in motioning Jamie not to upset Mary by revealing the possible extent of Edmund's illness. Tyrone then tries to allay Mary's fears, telling her of a certain Doctor Hardy's diagnosis. Mary nastily discredits Doctor Hardy, and Tyrone for consulting him. Tyrone avoids response by flattering Mary, who leaves in an insecurely happy mood to instruct the servants for the daily household business.

Tyrone attacks Jamie for his thoughtlessness in almost revealing to Mary the seriousness of Edmund's illness (which they both suspect is consumption). Jamie counters by excoriating Tyrone for his refusal to get the best possible treatment for Edmund. Tyrone counters by attacking Jamie for his lack of ambition, his lack of success in the theater, and for failing out of every school Tyrone had sent him to. Jamie attempts to counter but, bored, suddenly drops the argument. They turn to discussing Edmund's illness once more. Tyrone reveals that Doctor Hardy is to telephone his final diagnosis of Edmund during the lunch hour. Jamie accuses Tyrone of superstitiously believing as Irish peasants do that there is no hope for those stricken with consumption. The quarrel goes deeply into the past life of the characters, through a long series of recriminations. Tyrone accuses Jamie of having purposely tried to destroy Edmund by leading him into bad habits. During the course of the quarrel they both agree that Edmund has started what could turn out to be a promising career as a writer. Tyrone uses Edmund's success as a goad on Jamie. They then turn to an analysis of the mother and her prior "illness." They worry that Edmund's illness may bring back Mary's illness. They suspect she may already have started taking morphine again, but shamefacedly dismiss their suspicions. Jamie accuses Tyrone of having caused Mary's morphine habit by having hired a quack doctor to treat her for the pain she suffered after childbirth with Edmund, the same kind of cheap quack Tyrone is hiring for Edmund's illness.

Mary enters, interrupting their quarrel. They cover up and, after embarrassing Mary again by being overly concerned about her, go to cut the hedge in the yard. (Their concern seems to be not so much concern as accusation.)

Edmund enters. He and his mother joke about Tyrone's

penuriousness and Jamie's false pride. Mary bitterly complains that Tyrone has not provided her with the sort of home where she could carry on a normal social life. Edmund hints that her "illness" is partially to blame for the family's isolation. Mary complains that her family's overconcern about her makes her feel guilty and even more isolated. Then, strangely, she excuses herself for a "nap" to ease her tired nerves. Edmund, to prove he is not suspicious of what she may be up to, allows her to go upstairs unattended. He goes to watch Jamie at work.

This whole act has been a series of aborted quarrels about whether or not the past actions of the protagonists have been responsible for the present state of their characters.

## ACT II. SCENE 1

The same, around 12:45 P.M.
Edmund, alone, reads a book and glances apprehensively upstairs to where his mother had gone in the first act. Cathleen, the maid, brings in whiskey, banters familiarly with Edmund, and exits to shout loudly to Tyrone and Jamie to come up from the yard to lunch. Edmund furtively sneaks a drink, and Jamie enters. He too sneaks a drink, waters the whiskey to cover up, and the two brothers discuss Edmund's and Mary's illnesses. Jamie attacks Edmund for having allowed Mary to get out of his sight.

Mary enters, obviously under the influence of morphine, and attacks her two sons for the way they treat their father. Then she attacks Tyrone again for the shabby way of life he provides for her and for his family. Jamie accuses his mother of having relapsed into her habit, and Edmund and Jamie snarl at one another over this. Mary leaves.

Tyrone enters from the yard, and they begin to drink and bicker. Jamie hints sadistically that Tyrone himself will soon not be singing (when Tyrone discovers that Mary has succumbed to her morphine habit again).

Mary enters. She attacks Tyrone in her drug fog about the past life he has caused her to lead, with no decent home and no decent social life, because of his greed. She rambles on for quite some time, losing control, and only making disconnected sense, as Tyrone becomes aware of what has happened. The boys go into the dining room for lunch, leaving Tyrone and Mary alone. Tyrone brutally berates his wife for her "failure," and they go into lunch.

## ACT II. SCENE 2

The same, half an hour later.

Mary and the others enter, Mary still attacking Tyrone in her feverish manner about his greed having deprived them all of a decent home. Tyrone turns on her, but thinking better of it, gives up and lets her ramble on about the past. Doctor Hardy telephones. Tyrone answers the phone but does not say directly what Hardy's final report on Edmund is. The gloom of the family deepens, as Mary launches another hateful attack on Tyrone for his greed in not getting a better doctor for Edmund. Mary excuses herself, obviously to take another injection of morphine.

Jamie comments brutally on his mother, and Edmund and Tyrone turn on him snarlingly. Jamie counters with an attack on Edmund's reading habits. Tyrone attacks them both, exclaiming that the whole cause for their profligacy has been their turning from the Catholic faith. They regress with recriminations and accusations of one another into the past, as in the previous parts of the play. Their quarrels circle endlessly and pointlessly about past mistakes, and reveal or explain in these terms their present predicament. Tyrone announces that Doctor Hardy had told him on the phone that Edmund actually has consumption. Jamie attacks Tyrone for his evident hedging on getting the best possible treatment for Edmund. We continue to learn more about the past actions and present feelings of the characters.

Mary enters and they turn surreptitiously from the quarrel. Tyrone attempts to excuse himself so that he can dress and go into town with the boys. But Mary frantically tries to get him to stay with her until the boys return from dressing for town. Then a series of recriminations takes place. Mary accuses Tyrone further for his greed as she analyzes his past actions. Tyrone begs her to try to stop her habit. To excuse herself, she again dredges up things that Tyrone had done in the past. Finally she mentions her feeling that she had made a mistake in having married an actor and that the unsettled life Tyrone had caused her to lead (which he did not have to do, as he was very wealthy) has destroyed her socially. Mary directly recalls the quack Tyrone had hired to treat her for the pain she suffered after she had borne Edmund. Despite Tyrone's remonstrances, she also reveals her suspicion that Jamie as a child had purposely infected their dead baby son, Eugene, with measles by going into Eugene's room when both children had been left with Mary's mother, while Mary was improperly on tour with Tyrone. She then says that she should never have borne Edmund and connects her morphine habit, contracted while bearing Edmund, to a punishment for not having remained with Eugene in order to care for him properly. Tyrone constantly begs her to forget the past.

Edmund enters. Tyrone and Mary turn guiltily to small talk and false heartiness. Edmund makes a violent attack on his father, asking if Doctor Hardy had told him on the phone that he, Edmund, was going to die. Mary abuses Edmund, accusing him of malingering. Tyrone hushes her and embarrassedly excuses himself to get dressed. A sequence of mixed tenderness and hatred follows between Edmund and Mary. Edmund tries to get himself to ask his mother to make an attempt for his sake to stop the drug habit. But Mary foils this with attacks on him and a brutal accusation of her husband and two sons. Tyrone and Jamie come down into the hall and call Edmund from the living room, not even bothering to enter it. Edmund goes into the hall, and all three leave. As the scene ends Mary says:

> You're lying to yourself again. You wanted to get rid of them. Their contempt and disgust aren't pleasant company. You're glad they're gone.
> *She gives a little despairing laugh.*
> Then Mother of God, why do I feel so lonely?
> *Curtain.* (p. 95)

### ACT III

The same, 6:30 P.M.

This act opens with a very long scene between Cathleen, the maid, and Mary. Mary, apparently desperate for company, is plying her maid with whiskey. They relive the day, including Mary's trip to the druggist in the car (the *second-hand* one Tyrone had bought for her). They comment constantly on the foghorn and the foggy evening. The scene leads eventually into a retelling in full detail by Mary of her love for and life with Tyrone, the matinee idol. We learn fully her emotions on being swept off her feet as an innocent convent girl by Tyrone. This scene is simply a fuller revelation of how events in the past had shaped Mary's character.

Cathleen leaves. Tyrone and Edmund enter. Again the conversation circles around the past and how it has caused the present. We learn that Jamie won't be home, as usual, for dinner. Both Tyrone and Edmund have been drinking heavily, though they show few ill effects of it. Mary is quite lost in a fog of morphine. It is obvious that she really does not pay attention to what the men say. She continues dreamily recalling how the life of one-night stands in cheap hotels had destroyed the family and bitterly accusing Tyrone of greed, because he had enough money to avoid abusing his family in this way. The dead child, Eugene, is brought up again. The two men drink to soften the cutting analysis of the family's fate which Mary indulges herself in. Then she recalls the exact details of her wedding preparations for Tyrone, including her leaving of the convent. The conversation drifts back to the present briefly, involving recriminations about Mary's habit and her family's drinking and Tyrone's greed. Then, confusedly and clumsily, Tyrone and Edmund try to tell Mary that Edmund has consumption. But she will not listen and says cruel and hurtful things to Edmund, accusing him again of malingering. The quarrel becomes so violent that Edmund, stricken, leaves. Finally Mary admits to Tyrone she is aware of Edmund's serious condition. Tyrone attempts to get her to go in to dinner, but she frantically excuses herself, in order to take more morphine, but ostensibly to shield herself from the self-guilt and remorse her realization of Edmund's illness has caused. Tyrone moves wearily toward the dining room. Curtain.

## ACT IV

The same around midnight.

Tyrone, sitting alone in the darkened living room, is drinking himself into oblivion. Edmund stumbles in out of the foggy night, cursing his father for being too miserly to turn on the lights. The alcohol seems to increase the color and expressiveness of what the characters say to one another all during this act. There is much quotation from literature, and a sad expressiveness or nostalgia is evident in what the characters say. The quarrel over the lights continues in the most colorful tones, mock serious and tenderly cajoling. We discover that Jamie is in a brothel at the moment. Tyrone and Edmund indulge in a pointless and practically unplayed game of casino. During this card game the whole past of the two characters is gone into by both in great and poetic detail. The chief revelations are that Edmund has wanted to be a poet but has come to the conclusion through his travels and experience with his family that life is an absurd joke. We learn too that Tyrone's early poverty as a boy, his having had to support his whole family, has caused him to be obsessed with material goods in his later years. Eventually the other main facts are gone into more deeply: Jamie's profligacy, Tyrone's greed in having hired a quack for Mary after Edmund's birth which has caused her to become addicted to morphine, and the general decay and disintegration of all the family members. Tyrone also reveals that his greed had caused him to give up a great career as a Shakespearean actor, because he was making a great sum of money acting in the *Count of Monte Cristo* as Edmund Dantes, Dumas' hero. The points of conflict in the play are simply gone into in greater detail, until Jamie stumbles in, dead-drunk from the brothel. The recriminations continue in an even more scalding manner, until Jamie reveals that he actually has been jealous of Edmund and admits that he has tried to destroy him out of jealousy. Jamie then passes out. The recriminations continue at an almost insane pitch between Edmund and Tyrone, until they hear Mary come downstairs. Jamie wakes enough to say "The Mad Scene. Enter Ophelia!" (p. 170) Edmund strikes his brother fiercely. Mary enters, trailing her wedding dress, in a high pitch of feverish intensity, and plays out for them the exact moment of her years-before exit from the convent to marry Tyrone. Jamie recites from Swinburne almost in self-pity because of the spectacle his mother is *injuring them* with. The quarreling and bickering continue until Mary's final speech, which ends:

> That was in the winter of senior year. Then in the spring something happened to me. Yes, I remember. I fell in love with James Tyrone and was so happy for a time.

> *She stares before her in a sad dream. Tyrone stirs in his chair. Edmund and Jamie remain motionless.* (p. 176)

And so the play ends, with the final tragic fact of her character having been revealed in all its poignancy, as she recalls her first experience with love.

How shall we explain the peculiar power of this dramatic work? Something that has been happening throughout the play is suddenly made the exclusive focus of the fourth act. Two men, Tyrone and Edmund, father and son, sit at a table for practically three quarters of the fourth act and deliver an account of themselves to one another. After this, Jamie enters, accounts for himself primarily to Edmund, and then passes out. Edmund and Tyrone quarrel bitterly. Jamie wakens, joins momentarily in the quarrel, and then Mary enters. Talking to no one in particular, lost in the past, she gives an account of herself, and the play ends. Dull, you say? But at this point our tension as to why and how these people have become the warped and twisted things they are is at a great height, and the macabre qualities of their incidental behavior are almost hypnotic. The hour, the foghorn, the drunkenness, the morphine addiction, the stagey (false) quality of the appearance of their only "home," the grotesque aspects of their family relations, the lyrical quality of their speech, their shocking honesty in their final accounting of themselves to one another, and the heart-rending agony of their final unmasking of themselves, all, finally, contribute to creating in us and in them a mesmeric attention. For they *act out* in these final moments of the play the subconscious horrors they have angrily denied the existence of in the previous acts of the play. We get, as it were, a vivid image of those hatreds, loves, anxieties, and unacceptable motivations that lie in the most secret recesses of their personalities. And this dis-

play is all the more shocking because of the constant pointing in the previous dialogue to the existence of these
things in them that are finally revealed in all their naked
clarity.

We do not care what *happens* in terms of action or conflict. Let the two men sit at the table. Let the problems constantly elude solution. Let the larger world dissolve around
them. Let the very dialogue itself writhe to issue from
their mouths. Let the mother stumble absurdly into the
midst of the men's conversation. In short, let anything happen, so long as we can satisfy our craving to see into the
recesses of their hidden selves, to see displayed for us those
contorted inner drives of their personalities, which have
made them what they are.

The synthesizing material principle in this play is not
simply action. In our search for that principle, let us review
the many forces that are at work in the high climax of the
play's final moments in terms of our earlier list of principles that might form the synthesizing material center of a
play: emotion (passion), thought, character, fantasy, action, conflict, and so forth. Certainly all these elements are
present in this play. We shall be trying to discover if any
one or any combination of these principles seems to be
primary.

As the brief demonstrates, the dialogue of the four
protagonists circles in endless repetition around the four
key aspects of their condition: Mary's drug addiction, Edmund's illness, the profligacy of James, and the miserly
greed of Tyrone. These four dilemmas are hinted at in the
first dialogue of the play between Mary and Tyrone. The
*thought* applied by the protagonists to the dilemmas does
not progress very far toward any kind of solution. Furthermore, the *emotions* of the characters do not form a unifying center about which the drama coheres. The characters'
emotions are so varied, so much a product of the moment,

it is difficult to define them. An oral performance of practically any scene in the play demonstrates this for us.

This emotional ambivalence is at its height in the final scene of the play. Since there is a great preponderance of emotion emanating from the characters, we might mistake it for the central controlling material principle of the play. Therefore, let us examine this ambivalence in greater detail in order to discover whether it is either a unifying cause or an abundant effect which obscures a more primary principle.

Mary has just entered the living room in the final scene. She is even more deeply lost in her morphine jag than she had been in previous scenes. Tyrone, rather primly (a startling reaction to the evident pathos of Mary's predicament), relieves her of the wedding dress she is trailing behind her. She says she is looking for something, and Tyrone hopelessly appeals to her sense of, of all things, propriety. He seems not to be moved with pity at the disintegration of her character, but to be offended by her lack of "decent" behavior. He does not even rise from his chair to rush to her aid. He sits there beholding her final dissolution. Tyrone makes another appeal to her to stop. And what does her eldest son do, the one who evidently is most clearly attached to her, who throughout the play says he loves her most? He recites in a bath of self-pity lines from Swinburne's "A Leave-taking." She says again, pathetically, that she is looking for something she has lost. Still, none of them move from their chairs to comfort her. Yet they are concerned and moved for her, but they simply cannot forget themselves long enough to fly to her aid, to comfort her.

> JAMIE
> *Turns to look up into her face—and cannot help appealing pleadingly in his turn.*
> Mama!
> *She does not seem to hear. He looks away hopelessly.*

Hell! What's the use? It's no good.
> *He recites from "A Leave-taking" again with increased bitterness.*

"Let us go hence, my songs; she will not hear,
Let us go hence together without fear;
Keep silence now, for singing-time is over,
And over all old things and all things dear.
She loves not you nor me as all we love her.
Yea, though we sang as angels in her ear,
She would not hear." (p. 173)

When the interpreter gets down to the specific emotions of the characters arising from the actions of this scene, he soon becomes aware of its complex tensions, which are not fully evident in the denotative aspects of the words employed in the scene. The ambivalence of Jamie's emotions in delivering the Swinburne will become fully apparent if the interpreter begins reading all the roles aloud at Mary's entrance. He should keep in mind that the male speakers are heavily influenced by the effects of alcohol and that Mary's body is greatly affected by morphine. The alcohol and the physical tiredness allow the clear duality of Jamie's emotional attitude toward his mother (love-hate) to be expressed while he is reciting from Swinburne.

Within the context of the whole scene, as we project ourselves orally into these lines, we notice the emotions being pulled toward the mother, yet simultaneously the bitterness of the words themselves curbs the compassion that struggles to arise. This tension between the two emotions in the scene (love-hate) is never resolved. The compassion that struggles to arise in the characters is curbed through the bitterness of the words employed in the scene, such as those of Swinburne. The actions indicated in the stage directions call for either repressed physical movement or stasis and directly mirror the emotional impasse created by the words. Thus an evident dramatic effect of stalemate in the action is created in this scene. A terrible inertia seems to overcome the characters, so that after Mary's final speech the boys are motionless and Tyrone can only stir uneasily in his chair. It is on this note that the play ends, the note of an almost total dramatic impasse in the emotional relationships between the characters. The men are not even able to rise from their chairs. Even when they are about to raise the final drink of the play to their lips, the sudden recommencement of Mary's voice in her final speech causes them to lower their glasses to the table before they can drink. They sit, stunned, as does the audience, incapable of action, as this ambivalence of approach and withdrawal reaches its maximum, unresolved tension. And finally, most importantly for our investigation of this scene, because physical movement and emotional release have been all but annihilated by the emotional and physical stalemate between approach and withdrawal, we are forced to attend exclusively to the details of character Mary reveals.

It is illuminating to analyze Mary's love in terms of the realization that comes to T. S. Eliot's protagonist in *The Waste Land:* "Datta" (Give), "Dayadhvam" (Sympathize), "Damyata" (Control). Eliot's protagonist discovers that love consists not only of "giving" and of "sympathizing," but also of "controlling." Mary's love for Tyrone has been self-destructively inadequate. Mary has given too much, and therefore having so wrongfully deprived herself, she, like the rest of her family, but for a different reason, can no longer be connected with other human beings. She has not been able to "control," to give direction to, her husband and her sons, because her character is too weak. She cannot exercise "control," the proper "control" of her home situation, by curbing her husband's selfish desire to rear her children "on the road," so to speak, so that he can have her with him while he acts. She cannot find what she has lost, for in truth she never had it: strength of character.

Tyrone, on the other hand, has "control," strength of character, but he cannot "give" or "sympathize" and ends up as miserable as his wife. The two sons can neither "give" nor "control." They can only "sympathize." Their characters are lopsided, like the characters of their parents. They have a kind of selfish object-love, but cannot exercise "compassion," which must stem from a utilization of all three aspects of love: giving, sympathizing, and controlling.

If we were now to ask ourselves the question we asked previously, "How shall we explain the peculiar power of this dramatic work?" part of our answer would have to be "character," for it is apparently the primary material of which the play consists. The *material cause* of this play (the stuff out of which it is formed) seems to be character.

The central controlling material principle of this play seems to be the progressive revelation of character. From the first beat of the play, the characters undergo a progressive revelation which ends in the nadir of despair. The play may safely be described as a play of character, involving complete alteration in moral character, brought on and controlled by constantly stalemated actions and emotions, and made apparent in itself and in peripheral thought.

However, is it possible to state this synthesizing principle much more specifically and completely? The question with which we began, "How shall we explain the peculiar power of this dramatic work?" has been only partially answered by finding the material out of which the play has been formed. We have not as yet examined *all* the aspects of the play's form. We have merely discovered its primary material ingredient. As stated at the beginning of this essay, it is through arriving at some complete concept of form that we shall find a full answer to the question with which we began. It is, in other words, our response to the formal completeness of this play that may explain its peculiar aesthetic power. We have arrived at the *material* cause of the play, and in doing this we have answered the question, "Primarily what kind of human experience is the play imitating?" with "the experience of character."

In the Aristotelian scheme for the analysis of objects, there are three other causes of any object besides its *material* cause: *efficient, formal,* and *final.* Together, a knowledge of the relationships that exist between all four of the causal constituents of any object, including aesthetic objects, can serve to help us explain its peculiar power or *dynamis,* the effect of its form. All three of these other causes may be said to be subsumed under, or controlled by, an object's *formal* cause. The other three causes, *material, efficient,* and *final,* work within the limits set by the *formal* cause. Therefore, in order to study the form of an object such as a play, we cannot avoid having knowledge of the play's other three causes, if our description of the play's form is going to be a complete description.

If we are trying to fully explain the form of this object, *Long Day's Journey into Night,* we will have to begin asking questions about its other causes. We have pretty thoroughly answered the question about its material cause. But material has to be given a shape by someone, or some thing. The thing or person which gives material a shape can be called a producer, in the sense that we say, "He carves dolls out of wood." Wood is the material, and the producer is the carver. The man or thing that shapes the material can be called the producing agency, or the *efficient cause* of the object. In applying this to *Long Day's Journey into Night,* we are first led to say, "Well, Eugene O'Neill was the *efficient cause* or producing agency that produced this play." But since Eugene O'Neill is now dead, how can we possibly talk about the producing agency or *efficient cause* of this play's form? It is not really as difficult as it may appear. What we'll do is talk, not about Eugene O'Neill, but about something which Eugene O'Neill did, which has outlasted him and will probably outlast us. We can talk about the evidence of Eugene O'Neill's hand in the work. That will never disappear as long as the play remains. *What possibilities of the poetic material of character did Eugene*

*O'Neill select to employ in shaping Long Day's Journey into Night?* These selected possibilities of character still remain in the play for us to talk about, though O'Neill himself is dead. These selected possibilities of character, then, become the *efficient cause* of the play's form.

The possibilities of the poetic medium of character that O'Neill employed in this play again reside in the family relationships expressed in the play, as they did in *The Haunted,* the third play of his trilogy, *Mourning Becomes Electra.* But this play differs in three respects. The Tyrone family is a contemporary family, and the family members are not of so high a station in the community as were the Mannons; nor does the transgression of the family chain of command, in the form of the insubordination of the will of the individual to that familial order, progress so far as to *completely* break the chain of command within the family. The result is that physical violence is completely replaced with psychological violence in this play.

The play efficiently employs the possibility of character contained primarily in the defection of the father from a just pattern of familial order. Tyrone's greed causes him to usurp the mother's role of the distribution of goods within the family. His role should be that of acquiring necessary family commodities, but he attempts both roles. He is the "breadwinner." He provides very sufficient funds, earned through his brilliant acting career, to support a family in very comfortable style. But the portioning out of this money and the goods it buys to feed and clothe the family, to house it, and to pay for schooling and recreation is also taken over by Tyrone. Mary complains bitterly of his performance in this regard, as do his sons. Tyrone acquires *and* distributes. This leaves the mother, Mary, deprived of one of her most necessary functions, the distribution of goods within the family. This, in turn, affects the two children, Edmund and James. Because of the frustration imposed on her by Tyrone, Mary is unable to provide the proper sort of home atmosphere in which to train her sons. They, in turn, lacking a stable home environment in which to develop, are not able to make productive contacts with the world at large, which they both obviously fear and mistrust, as a result of the fear and mistrust they have learned to have for their family situation. Tyrone's greed indirectly causes, or extends, the psychological wound already inflicted on Mary, when in his penuriousness he has her attended by an inferior physician, who gives her large doses of morphine which develop into a drug habit. Tyrone's greed, then, is the key to the disintegration apparent in himself and in each member of his family.

Mary, as a character, lacks sufficient moral fiber to regain the role of a distributor of goods within the family. Her very infatuation with Tyrone, whom she had loved romantically and unquestioningly in the beginning, does not allow her to exert sufficient force against him to correct his usurpation of her role as distributor of goods within the family. It is her very innocence, her sweetness of temper, her long-suffering qualities, that further contribute to the gradual disintegration of the proper hierarchy of authority within the family. Mary's very gentleness of character, as the play presents her, is her greatest liability. Not having the force of character to assert her just motherly authority within the home, she retreats progressively from the present into the past. Her escape into morphine is not the primary causal factor of her retreat from the present into the past. The escape into the drug is merely an extension of her prior retreat from the responsibility of maintaining her role of establishing the proper sort of home environment for the rearing of her children. This is not supposition, for Mary *knows quite consciously* what her defects of character are when she says:

> I blame only myself. I swore after Eugene died I would never have another baby. I was to blame for his death. If I hadn't left him with my mother to join you on the

road, because you wrote telling me you missed me and
were so lonely, Jamie would never have been allowed,
when he still had measles, to go in the baby's room.
(p. 87)

Jamie, having constantly lacked the reference to a just
point of authority in the family, either patriarchal or matri-
archal, seeks only disorganized relationships in the world at
large. Mary knows what is wrong with Jamie (as well as
knowing what is wrong with herself, Tyrone, and Edmund) when she says further along in the above-quoted
speech:

I've always believed Jamie did it on purpose. He was
jealous of the baby. He hated him.
   *As Tyrone starts to protest.*
Oh, I know Jamie was only seven, but he was never
stupid. He'd been warned it might kill the baby. He
knew. I've never been able to forgive him for that.
(p. 87)

We discover later that Jamie hates and loves Edmund,
hates him against his own will, for, never having been *sure*
of equitable love and direction from his parents, he hates
anything that threatens what little attention he does get
from them. Paradoxically, it is his very need for love, and
the control that goes with it, that drives him to take re-
venge on the world for what his parents have not given
him. Jamie knows this and states it clearly to Edmund:

Never wanted you to succeed and make me look even
worse by comparison. Wanted you to fail. Always jealous of you. Mama's baby, Papa's pet! (p. 165)

Edmund, despite the damage done to his character, has
succeeded in partially breaking from the family disorder
and has at least attempted positive and independent action.
He writes and publishes poetry. He started writing and

publishing after a period of aimless wandering and an attempted suicide. He is now seriously ill, but his restraint, his desire to understand himself and the other characters, is a continuing and positive force within the play.

The possibilities of the poetic medium of character O'Neill chose to select and imitate in this play may be summarized in the following manner. A family of characters is imitated in the play, in which the father has usurped, through greed, the distributive function of the mother, who is herself too weak to reëstablish her proper authority. The father's usurpation and the mother's weakness in the face of it produce two sons, one of them, Jamie, completely unable to relate to the larger world in any truly productive way, and the other, Edmund, only partially able to relate to the larger world in a productive way. Further, all the characters are essentially aware of what their individual character flaws happen to be; but only two of them, Mary and Edmund, have significant insight into what is wrong with the others. Tyrone knows that he is greedy, but will not accept the fact that this has ruined his family. Jamie knows that he hates, but will not accept total responsibility for his hatred.

We have now answered two questions about the form of this play: (1) primarily what kind of human experience is this play imitating? and (2) through the selection of what possibilities of the poetic material has the experience been imitated? But an object, as we have stated earlier, has more than two causes, *material* and *efficient*. It also has a *formal* cause and a *final* cause.

In getting at a description of the *formal* cause of the play our task is relatively less complex than the two previous tasks of describing the *material* and *efficient* causes. The formal cause of this play fulfills the general condition for what we call drama: actors speaking lines on a stage. To be more specific, however, we will have to attempt to describe the dramatic mode, the special kind of dramatic *form* O'Neill imposed on his material and its specially selected qualities.

We may phrase the question in this way: *Into what mode of dramatic representation have the selected possibilities of the material of character been formed?* Looking again at our brief of the play, we can see that the dramatic mode of this play is slightly different from that of, say, *Desire Under the Elms* or O'Neill's other naturalistic plays. Up to a certain point, the dialogue in prose depends primarily on the evocation of casually selected realistic surfaces; but in the final act, a heavily textured prose, interspersed with long quotations from verse, is employed. The dialogue at this point becomes more lyrical (mirroring a rich subjective emotion in the characters) than in any of O'Neill's other plays, with the exception perhaps of *The Hairy Ape*. The plot, in the sense of the structure of events, in this play is clearly a *simple plot,* which means that the action is one continuous whole, with neither a complete reversal of the protagonists' fortunes nor any discovery of previously unrevealed facts of the protagonists' pasts (if the structure of events did contain these things it excludes, it would be called a *complex plot*). There appears to be no supersubtle selection of detail for special effects.

We have now answered three of the four questions raised by our original question which was, "How shall we explain the peculiar power of this dramatic work?" If we look at the play as an object built of language in a certain way, the answer to our question must include precise answers to questions about *all* significant aspects of the object which are subsumed within its *formal* cause, even though our analysis centers about the object's form, or formal cause. As we have said previously, we'll have to talk about the *material* of which the object is made, the possibilities of the material which have been *efficiently* selected to go into the specific object of which we are talking, the *form* which is wrought from the efficiently selected possibilities of the material, and, finally, the *purpose* or *end* the object has been formed or wrought to serve, its *final* cause.

This fourth kind of question about the purpose or end for which the form has been shaped is the most difficult and complex of the four questions we are asking ourselves about the formal nature of the aesthetic object, *Long Day's Journey into Night*. The more complex the object, the more complex the end to which it may be employed becomes. Objects created *in* language, which employ its semantic units in the construction of a basic material such as imitated experience, are perhaps the most complex objects imaginable. We usually are not aware of this complexity, because we use language every day of our existence and language seems perhaps less foreign to most of us in terms of its complexity than any other kind of symbolic instrument we use. It goes without saying that no machine could ever be as complex as language itself. This is true even of the legendary computer. A very wise man once said of the computer, when it was suggested to him that computers might some day be taught to write poems, "Well, I suppose that would be possible; but don't you think that the only readers of such poems would be computers?" It appears, at this point in time, that computers will never be more complex than the men who program them, whereas the possibilities within language and its continuous use and change are practically infinite. With this in mind, let us ask our final question, remembering that our answer is probably going to be very complex.

We may phrase our question in this way: *For the purpose of evoking and controlling what particular sequence of emotions and expectations is the experience of character being imitated (in relation to the successive parts of the imitation)?* Answering this fourth question, concerning the sequence of expectations and emotions that are clearly evoked in the characters themselves, and hence in us by the play, will require that we describe those emotions and expectations in the specific temporal order in which they occur in the play. Since we cannot reduce or simplify this answer into a "meaning," we are going to have to present it for purposes of convenience and clarity in a very unsentencelike form.

Referring to our brief of the play, we can see that the sequence of emotions and expectations proceed generally thus: Act I, amusement—curiosity; amused worry—difficulties; anxiety—disruption. Act II, scene 1, fear—backsliding of Mary; disappointment—further disruption; pity and regret—dissolution of Mary; scene 2, deeper gloom and depression—further dissolution of Mary and hospitalization of Edmund; pity and horror—total disruption of family. Act III, nostalgic regret—understanding; pity and horror—total disruption and dissolution of family. Act IV, hope and compassion—resolution; horror—catastrophe; suspense and compassion—resolution and understanding.

When thus we come to look directly at the question of the purpose of the play in regard to the sequence of emotions and expectations it appears to evoke in the characters and in us, we find that suspense has been almost entirely replaced by another effect, cumulative revelation of character. It is the gradual filling in of the details of character, pretty well established from the beginning of the play, that holds our attention. This is similar to the effect of suspense, but is, at the same time, significantly different. It is the cumulative knowledge about the characters revealed to us through their analysis of themselves and one another that fairly rivets our attention in this play. We know approximately what they are from the outset. As the play progresses, their characters are progressively revealed in increasingly accumulated detail. And the more we come to know about the characters through their speech and action, the more we pity them, with the pity of comprehension or perception that gradually increases our awareness of why they are what they have become. The thing that makes the pity increasingly painful to bear is the fact that the potential in the characters for having become something other than what they are is made clear at every step of the progressive character revelation.

If only Mary had asserted her motherly authority within the family; if only Tyrone had supplanted his greed by love at critical moments; if only the sons had changed emotional rebellion into industry when the few proper chances were offered them. It is the appalling waste of human potential that so moves us. But this progressive state of knowledge is also an intrinsic part of the development and exposition of each character.

The overwhelming effect in the play exists in the comparative lack of dramatic irony (wherein the audience knows more than the characters speaking). As the characters reveal more about themselves, the audience, moving exactly parallel with the characters' revelations, discovers more, too. This has the effect of erasing the distance between the audience and the characters, as the characters discover that it is not fate in the external sense that has so affected them, but their own actions, for which they are directly responsible. The universality of Mary's revelation of why her loss of innocence has destroyed her is the final climactic effect in this regard. We learn that she has been destroyed by her loss of innocence through the experience of unqualified love for the first time, her love for Tyrone. And the experience is so close to the universal experience of mankind that finally we are drawn into a complete identification with her and the other characters.

But, oddly enough, it is Mary, at this point, through the aid of the drug, who has something comparable to an aesthetic distance from the revelation about herself. We, the audience, are the ones who have little or no protection from the poignancy of the revelation, and it is just this that makes

Mary's final speech so overwhelmingly powerful in its effect upon us. We have become identified with her, but she is insulated from the awful force of this knowledge, the effect of the drug having given her sufficient protection from the tragic fact of her existence. In this sense, the play leads us not only to a discovery of an aspect of Mary's character, but also to the discovery of an aspect of our own experience.

What the play is, as an aesthetic object, must be what endows it with such power. Now we are prepared to construct an *inducted description* of that aesthetic object, the play. In relation to *our* perception, the play is a stimulus, not a response. When we shall have discretely described the stimulus, we shall be better prepared to explain our response and to answer our original question: "How shall we explain the peculiar power of this dramatic work?"

If we combine the essentials of the answers to our four questions of fact, we arrive at the following formal description of this play, wherein we now see the material cause, the efficient cause, and the final cause as contributory to the *dynamis* of the piece, the effect arising from its form, or, in the fullest sense, its formal cause. The formal cause (in our case dramatic) is that which determines the mode in which a thing exists or is perceived.

*Long Day's Journey into Night* is a drama of character, involving a progressive and thorough revelation of moral character (not, as was originally hypothesized, *a complete alteration*), brought on and controlled by psychological tensions that stalemate action, and made apparent in itself and in peripheral thought. The character of a father who has usurped the distributive functions of the mother, through his own greed, is revealed through the imitation, along with a mother too weak to regain her lost authority and unable to provide a stable home environment for the two sons, whose characters are also revealed. The elder son is revealed as completely unable to establish productive relationships in society, while the younger son is revealed as a character who, though damaged by the family situation, is able to relate to the larger world of society productively, though in a limited way. The dramatic mode consists primarily of an imitation of casual realistic surfaces in ordinary prose dialogue, until the fourth act, in which the dialogue becomes heavily lyrical and the speeches of the characters become steeped in an introspective subjectivity. All of this is accomplished with a simple plot structure of events. With the gradual revelation of character, two effects are achieved: the effect of suspense is replaced by the parallel acquisition of character knowledge on the part of the characters and the audience; this, in turn, erases the distance between the audience and the characters, allowing thorough identification of the audience with the characters. When the final tragic fact (that Mary's unqualified love for Tyrone has destroyed her moral integrity) is revealed, the conventional roles of the audience and of the characters have essentially been reversed; for the characters, through the aid of alcohol and morphine, have established an even greater distance from the poignancy of the tragic fact than that distance which is conventionally the sole prerogative of the audience.

The above paragraph, a description of the form wrought from certain selected possibilities inherent in a certain kind of material, which has been wrought to serve a complex, though describable end, should not be mistaken for the object itself, *Long Day's Journey into Night*. We should not mistake either our method of analysis or the conclusion it allows for the drama itself. Our formal description is an empirically inducted *hypothesis* that attempts to describe the unique nature of one particular drama. And as is the case with all truly synthetic propositions (deriving from observed facts), it does not claim absolute finality. Instead, it awaits further testing by observation, and most probably continuing change and refinement by successive groups of observers. The object is of sufficient complexity to demand an invitation to further study, and hence further refinement of the hypothesis which attempts to describe it. This inductive method of analysis has the further advantage of being like the condition of learning itself, which is, we hope, dynamic, not static.

# III

Ideally, the way to begin the oral study of literature is to apply the oral method at the outset. This is a convenient method to apply to the lyric; less convenient but quite possible with the drama; and, admittedly, rather unwieldy with the novel, but nonetheless convenient for the short story. But within the limits of common sense, we should very early, through reading the whole piece, or passages of it, aloud, put the actual scenes so far as possible before our eyes and act out the piece with the very gestures of the personages contained in it.

Form in literature consists of the describable relationship between content and the manner in which that content has been structured. Consequently, in perceiving the form of a piece, we are not primarily trying to acquire meanings; we are trying to perceive how the formal cause of the piece orders and subsumes its content into itself: how the material of the piece, the efficient structuring of that material, and the purpose or end for which the efficient structuring of the material has been accomplished synthesize themselves or relate themselves into the piece's form. We therefore concern ourselves with causal factors rather than exclusively with semantic factors, though semantic factors are a *part* of our concern. We proceed inductively, that is, from particular to general statements (as in our brief), and treat each poem, lyric, play, novel, as a unique individual insofar as possible.

First we construct a brief, a series of observation statements about the symbolic activity we observe in the text.

Then we ask ourselves four questions about the symbolic activity we have observed:

1. Primarily what kind of human experience is the poem imitating?

2. Primarily what possibilities of that kind of human experience does the poem efficiently select?

3. Primarily what form (mode of representation) have the efficiently selected possibilities of the experience been wrought into?

4. Primarily for the purpose of evoking what particular sequence of emotions and expectations have the selected possibilities of that kind of human experience been wrought into that particular mode of representation?

Having constructed our brief, asked the four questions, and answered them, we then combine our answers into a synthesis that attempts to describe how the form of the piece orders or subsumes its material, the efficient structuring of its material, and its final end or purpose into its form.

Any object, including an aesthetic object, can be analyzed from the standpoint of its form. But in order to fully describe such an object's form, we must describe the material in its form, the efficient structuring of that material within its form, and the purpose this efficient structuring of the material serves within the object's form. Only then can the way in which a thing exists, takes shape, or shows itself (in our case, dramatically) be *fully* perceived as a formal entity. That is why our formal description of the object has included a description of its material, efficient, and final causes. All of these causes operate, or inhere, within the object's formal cause and the consequent *dynamis*, working power, or effect peculiar to that form.

As was said at the outset of this essay, *when we train ourselves to perceive the form of a piece of literature, we are indulging in a contemplative mode of behavior, not in an acquisitive one. As the perception of beauty occasions*

89

*what appears to be a moment of perception detached from desire or action, wherein the senses of sight, touch, taste, hearing, and movement are extended into the pattern of the object which is being perceived, so does the perception of form.*

## RECOMMENDED READING

The method of formal analysis I have illustrated for you in analyzing *Long Day's Journey into Night* is a reduced, systematic, and simplified method. And while it loses some value in detail, it is nevertheless a method that can be employed by the undergraduate with the assistance of his instructor. Like any other method of analysis, it requires practice and patient application to be successful. But it is a hypothetical analysis, and the hypothesis of formal synthesis which is its end product is not considered to contain any sacred or absolute truth. Such hypotheses invite constant improvement, revision, and additions and subtractions, and continued testing against the observable facts in the text. It is a conditional method and requires great patience. Its yield of information depends (1) on the suspension of judgment until it is completed and (2) on the willingness to painstakingly revise any part of it that does not fit in with new discoveries on the part of the analyzer or the performers who look at the text being analyzed. It is, however, dynamic and depends on the *participation* of the student for greatest success. It is also of particular use to the oral student of literature because (1) it invites the magnified view of the oral performance and (2) it provides a view of the whole form, which it is the special province of the interpreter to embody in his performance.

You may wish to refer to professional examples of the method's application to the narrative and the lyric. For the narrative you may wish to read Ronald S. Crane's "The Concept of Plot and the Plot of *Tom Jones*," in the inexpensive paperback, *Critics and Criticism,* Ronald S. Crane, ed., abridged ed. (Chicago: Phoenix, 1957), pp. 62-93. For the lyric you may read Elder Olson's essay, "'Sailing to Byzantium': Prolegomena to a Poetics of the Lyric," in Wilbur Scott, ed., *Five Approaches of Literary Criticism,* (New York: Macmillan, 1963), pp. 215-230.

For extended study of this method you may wish to refer to the definitive work on the subject, R. S. Crane's *The Languages of Criticism, and the Structure of Poetry* (Toronto: University of Toronto, 1953). Having read Crane's extension of Aristotle's principles to fit modern literature, you may want to turn to Aristotle's treatise itself. An excellent modern translation, quoted from at the beginning of the present essay, is Ingram Bywater's, in Richard McKeon, ed., *Introduction to Aristotle* (New York: Random House, 1947), pp. 624-667.

For a more general treatment of the nature and function of literature you may want to refer to René Wellek's and Austin Warren's *Theory of Literature,* 3rd ed. (New York: Harvest, 1963).

For further study of the critical use of language as a tool of analysis in the deductive (analytic) and inductive (synthetic) modes, you may wish to refer to Alfred Jules Ayer's *Language Truth and Logic* (New York: Dover, 1964). And for further general study in aesthetic concepts, you may wish to refer to *The Great Ideas, A Syntopicon,* Mortimer J. Adler, ed., in *Great Books of the Western World* (Chicago: Encyclopaedia Britannica, 1952). The article, "Beauty," pp. 112-125, in this work is particularly instructive, and is extensively cross-referenced.

For further study of O'Neill's dramatic forms, you may wish to refer to Chester C. Long's *A Study of the Role of Nemesis in the Plays of Eugene O'Neill* (The Hague, The Netherlands: Mouton & Company, to be published shortly).

## Projects

1. Construct a formal analysis of some other drama with which you are familiar. Then, select a scene that illustrates the material principle of the form of the drama you have chosen, i.e., character, action, thought, passion, fantasy, and so on. Be prepared to read this scene aloud. As part of your formal analysis or as a separate essay, discuss your selected scene by concentrating primarily on any aspects in the scene that you had not noticed in previous readings:

   a. List these new aspects.
   b. Indicate how they influence your perception of the emotional tone of the scene.
   c. Indicate how they influence your handling of the physical and vocal qualities suggested by the scene, such as gesture, quality, force, pitch, rate.
   d. Indicate how they influence your performance of imagery in the scene. Do you notice yourself having a more vivid response to some of the images than to others on the basis of these new insights?
   e. Do you find particular lines of dialogue taking on a new significance?

2. Construct a formal analysis of a short story with which you are familiar. Then, on the basis of the efficient principle of the form of the short story you have chosen, select a passage of the narrative and prepare it to be read aloud. As part of your formal analysis or as a separate essay, discuss your selected passage by concentrating primarily on any new aspects in the passage you had not noticed in previous readings:

   a. List these new aspects.
   b. Indicate how they influence your perception of the narrator's attitude toward his story.
   c. Indicate how they influence your handling of the

physical and vocal qualities suggested by the passage, such as gesture, quality, force, pitch, rate.

d. Indicate how they influence your performance of imagery in the passage. Do you notice the narrator indulging in the use of certain key kinds of imagery?

e. Do you find particular aspects of the narrator's technique, simple things such as "he said," taking on a new significance?

3. Construct a formal analysis of a lyric with which you are familiar. Then, prepare it to be read aloud. In writing your analysis, pay particular attention to any new aspects of the lyric you have not noticed in previous readings:

a. List these new aspects.

b. Indicate how they influence your perception of the lyric speaker's emotional state.

c. Indicate how they influence your handling of the physical and vocal qualities suggested by the lyric, such as gesture, quality, force, pitch, rate.

d. Indicate how they influence your performance of figures of speech and imagery in the lyric. Do you notice the lyric speaker indulging in the use of particular sequences of figures and images?

e. Do you find particular aspects of lyric technique, things such as personal references and subjective perceptions, taking on new significances?

# CHAPTER THREE

# LINGUISTIC ANALYSIS:

## A Study of
## James Mason's Interpretation of
## "The Bishop Orders His Tomb"

*SEYMOUR CHATMAN*

## I

Linguistics is a considerable subject and only partly relevant to oral interpretation. A useful division has been made into three parts: prelinguistics, linguistics proper, and paralinguistics. Prelinguistics is phonetics, the study of speech sounds in general, without reference to how they work in specific languages. The phonetician studies the anatomy of the voice—the way in which speech sounds are formed or how the ear receives them. Or he studies speech sounds as acoustic events similar to other acoustic events in nature: explosions, music, street noises.

Distinguished from phonetics is phonology, the most basic branch of linguistics proper. Phonology is the study of speech sounds *within* languages. Its fundamental unit is the phoneme. Phonemes serve specific purposes within a language's structure: they are building blocks which form larger units, such as words and sentences. We distinguish between two kinds of phonology: segmental and nonsegmental. The segmental phonemes are those that appear separately and in sequence in the chain of speech—for instance, /p/, /r/, /v/, /uː/, and so forth. (Slant lines are used to show that we are referring to phonemes and not mere letters.) Another kind of phoneme is the nonsegmental phoneme, sometimes called "suprasegmental" because of the linguist's custom of presenting his notation *above* the segmental phonemes. Another term is "prosodic." Nonsegmental phonology considers vocal features which occur at the same instant as segmental phonemes and which add to the meanings conveyed by them. For example, there is stress: stress must be phonemic—an element in the phonology—because in and of itself it can distinguish two words whose other phonemes are identical. Compare, for example, the words *billow* versus *below* or *fore-bears* versus *forbears*. A syllable is usually marked as stressed by a combination of at least three phonetic factors: greater length, greater loudness, and characteristic pitch change. Another feature in the nonsegmental phonology is intonation or sentence melody. Every utterance is spoken in one of a limited number of tunes, and different meanings are systematically correlated with these tunes. An obvious example is the difference marked by rise or fall at the ends of sentences. For example, an utterance ordinarily marked as a statement by a final fall, like

You're com
$^{ing}$

may be turned into a question by using a final rise, instead.

You're com
$^{ing}$

Another function of intonation, to signal attitudes and emotions, is paralinguistic and will be discussed later.

The other subdivision of linguistics proper is grammar. Grammar plays only a marginal role in interpretation, since the interpreter ordinarily is not the author of what he is reading, and even if he were, he would then have been functioning in another role. But grammar implies characteristic intonations, and the interpreter is, of course, obliged to pick the correct ones. For example, one must raise one's voice in a question like *you're coming?* or read long modifying phrases rapidly and with falling intonations after their heads to be sure they can be connected with what precedes rather than with what follows. Note the amusing consequences of not doing so:

What's that down the road a $^{h}e_{a}{}_{d}$

What's that down the $^{r}o_{a}{}_{d}$ $_{a}he^{a}{}^{d}$

Beyond linguistics proper is "paralinguistics," whose relevance to oral interpretation is very apparent. Paralinguistics includes all those vocal features which are more or less *phonetically* identifiable but which are not *linguistic* in the narrower sense, features which are less systematic, less easily pinned down to specific meanings than are the elements of linguistic structure per se. Their function, too, is different: they are more likely to tell something about the *speaker* than to contribute to his *literal message.* One can take a bare message—that neutral, writeable essence—and vary it in many ways in terms of differing nonlinguistic but situationally relevant factors, like the speaker's age, his sex, his general physical make-up, his present state of health, his feelings of the moment, often his social class and place of residence, and perhaps even his profession. I call them "factors" because I can't quite call them meanings. Linguistic features *refer* to things and actions, whereas paralinguistic features *identify:* they don't *stand for* something but are rather characteristic of the speaker himself. An old man's sounding like an old man is no less a part of him than the wrinkles on his brow—his voice is less a symbol than a *sign* of his age, if we make that useful distinction between signs as *parts of* the stimulus and symbols as separate entities *standing for* the stimulus. In this sense, a word, say, *cat,* is not made of the same stuff as that to which it refers—it is a symbol. But the soft timbre of a gentle woman's voice is a sign, a part and an identifier of her total make-up.

The analysis of paralanguage is difficult because of the impalpability of the features, the difficulty of extracting them from the total communication, our kinesthetic insensitivity to the movements of the vocal mechanism, particularly the parts down in the back of the throat, and the limited vocabulary which tradition has bequeathed us for describing such things. But some features have been more or less clearly identified. For example: (1) general pitch range, that is, the relative height of the voice, the extent to which it goes up or down; (2) vocal cord control, the extent to which the voice rasps or sounds clear; (3) glottis control, the extent to which the voice sounds breathy; (4) pitch control, the way in which the voice proceeds from one pitch point to the next, that is, sharply or smoothly; (5) articulation control, the relative precision or tension with which the upper parts of the vocal apparatus—tongue, teeth, and so forth—form segmental sounds, ranging from forceful to relaxed or sloppy; (6) rhythm control, the relative smoothness or jerkiness with which speech moves through time; (7) resonance, roughly the fullness or hollowness of the voice; and (8) tempo, the relative speed at which the syllables follow along. The term *control* means "in the domain of," rather than "possessing the conscious ability to manipulate," for people differ in their capacity to vary the effect of these mechanisms. For example, most of us can change our general patterns of articulation fairly easily; we can imitate a drunkard by generally loosening the tension of the front organs, turning our *"s's"* into *"sh's,"* for instance. But it takes some training, the training that actors receive in good acting schools, to learn to alter vocal cord movements, for instance, to manipulate one's larynx and adjacent organs for the breathy hoarseness and gravelly quality typical of the speech of old people. (The performance by James Mason, analyzed below in part II, provides a good illustration.) It is to be noted that these terms are physiological rather than auditory. They refer to what one does with his voice, rather than what one hears someone else do. Terms of auditory impression are well known but much vaguer—we hear of thick voices and thin, flat and vibrant, clear and dull, bright and dark, and so forth. There are other nonspeech effects which can be clearly labeled: laughing and its relatives giggling and snickering; crying (including whimpering and sobbing); yelling; whispering and muttering; moaning, groaning, and whining; breaking, belching, and yawning; overloudness and oversoftness, overheight and overlowness; and drawling and clipping.

One can also make a neat distinction according to the *functions* which paralinguistic features perform. They serve, first, to *identify* the speaker and, second, to convey his *feelings and attitudes* toward himself, his auditor, or the general environment, attitudes which need not be communicated by the literal message which he is uttering. In fact, there may be a discrepancy between the literal message and the attitude, as when someone says how glad he is to see us, and we know from the tone that he is lying.

Let us consider an example. A speaker identifies himself, say, as a specific old man (he is who he is—say, John Jones—by characteristic voice quality, and he is old by vocal breathiness and rasp, relaxed articulation, thin resonance, low pitch range, and slow tempo). At the same time, he shows himself to be, say, a poor Southerner (by the particular choice of segmental phonemes characteristic of the dialect, for example, /a/ instead of /ai/ in a word like "fine"), who is tired and fat (by puffing, uneven rhythms, and so on). A good way to think of identificational features is as that part of a radio actor's voice which helps us distinguish him from the other actors in the play even though we can't see him. It is interesting to note that some features (like those conveying identity, sex, age) are partly physiological and partly learned from the culture, while others (like place of residence, class, and so forth) are entirely learned and have nothing to do with the physiological shape of one's voice. That is why the latter are so much easier to imitate.

Second, paralinguistic features convey feelings and attitudes, and this function may be so important in the total communication as seriously to modify or even contradict the literal message. How often we say of a person that we didn't mind so much what he said as the way he said it. One can call someone a fool in so charming a way as to convey affection and warmth; or one can call a man a genius and make it sound like an insult. The signaling of attitude is primarily the function, the *other* major function, of intonation. Experiments which have recently been made of attitude-marking intonations should interest the oral interpreter. It has been shown that there is a significant difference in response to a wide, as compared to a narrow, intonational spread, that is, the range from highest to lowest tone. Wide-ranging questions sound pleasant and interested, narrow-ranging questions unpleasant and uninterested. Compare, for example,

$$\text{Did}\quad{}^{\text{you see}}\quad\text{him?}$$

and

$$\text{Did you s}^{\text{ee}}\text{ him?}$$

Wide-ranging statements and commands sound authoritative, while narrow-ranging statements sound submissive.

Compare

I $^{\text{want}}$ $_{\text{you}}$ $_{\text{to}}$ do $^{\text{th}}$$^{\text{at}}$

and

I want you to do th$^{\text{at}}$

The rise or fall of final syllables conveys different implications. Final rises in questions tend to sound pleasant, for example,

Won't $_{\text{you}}$ $^{\text{go?}}$

Final falls without preceding changes in direction sound uninterested,

Won't you $_{\text{go?}}$

and final falls *with* preceding changes in direction sound distinctly unpleasant.

Won't $^{\text{you}}$ $_{\text{go?}}$

In commands, final rises sound interested and at the same time submissive or deferential to one's auditor. Compare

Please $_{\text{do}}$ it.

with

Please $^{\text{do}}$ it.

In statements, final rises tend to give a greater impression of interest than do falls, which are generally noncommittal. Compare

He seems like a nice fel$^{\text{l}}$$^{\text{ow.}}$

with

He seems like a nice $^{\text{fel}}$$_{\text{low.}}$

Rises in statements, of course, have other implications as well, perhaps the strongest being indecision or concession.

English speakers also seem to respond differently to utterances according to whether contours are smooth or broken, that is, whether the unstressed syllables are on the same level as the stressed syllables which surround them. An example will clarify. Try the statement first with a smooth contour:

The policeman is standing on the <sup>cor</sup>ner.

The policeman is standing on the corner.

Notice that the weak syllables—*the, po-, -man, is, -ing, on,* and *the*—are all on the same level as the stressed syllables next to them. In the next version, *raise* the weak syllables so that they are above their adjacent strong syllables:

The pol<sub>i</sub><sub>ce</sub> man is <sub>stand</sub>ing on the cor<sub>ner</sub>.

This configuration in statements sounds distinctly less pleasant to our ears—the effect is one of condescension and impatience. Contrast with this the pleasant and interested sounding pattern in which the unstressed syllables are *lower* than the stressed:

The po<sup>lice</sup> man is <sup>stand</sup>.ing on the <sup>cor</sup>ner.

This sketch suggests some possible applications of linguistic and paralinguistic knowledge to the interpreter's art. What of that art itself, from the linguistic point of view?

In his effort to create or re-create a poem orally with vividness and accuracy, what can the interpreter do? What are the speech mechanisms available to him? Obviously, they are entirely phonological. Indeed, only a part of the phonology is available, for he cannot alter the sequence of segmental phonemes without altering the words themselves. As far as segmental phonology is concerned, all he can do is to select one among a small number of alternative phonemes to represent a local dialect (or more rarely, bodily condition or the like). The use or nonuse of dialect, of course, is a complex matter of taste in its own right. The demands are fairly obvious in interpreting *Brer Rabbit* or the *Bigelow Papers* or Mark Twain's "Jumping Frog," but what about the poems of Robert Frost or John Crowe Ransom? Once we have heard these poets read, we can hardly imagine their poems outside the context of New England or Southern speech; but should interpreters also use dialectical pronunciations? These are knotty interpretational questions, which the linguist is relieved to be able to pass back to the oral interpreter. All the linguist can do is to present the phonological facts, to point out that dialect is characteristically marked by a certain selection of segmental phonemes (although other factors, like tempo, are also involved), and to remark that the interpreter or actor who is good at dialects has learned how to make the proper substitutions, to say /næU/ instead of /naU/ for "now," and /ta:d/ instead of taIrd/ for "tired," to represent Southern speech; to say /dans/ instead of /dæns/ for "dance," and /təld/ instead of /əərd/ for "third," to suggest Brooklynese; to say /meri:/ instead of /mæri:/ for "Mary," and /pak/ instead of /park/ for "park," to suggest the dialect of the Back Bay.

As for the utilization of suprasegmental phonology, by far the most important of the interpreter's control, it is useful to think of three separate tasks of ascending sophistication and difficulty. The first is communicating the syntax. The second is identifying the *persona.* The third is conveying the appropriate attitudes and feelings in the appropriate places.

Communicating the syntax is the most elementary problem in interpretation, a kind of *sine qua non* of recitation. What shall we call it? *Syntax-clarification* is the best term I can find, the art of rendering audibly transparent the grammatical structure of a discourse. This is the *clarificational* function of oral interpretation, as opposed to the *identificational* and the *emotional*. What makes for good syntax-clarification? The problem seems largely one of intonation and timing.

Take, for example, the following part of Satan's speech in the second book of Milton's *Paradise Lost*:

> Me though just right and the fixed laws of Heav'n
> Did first create your Leader, next, free choice,
> With what besides, in Counsel or in Fight,
> Hath been achiev'd of merit, yet this loss
> Thus far at least recover'd, hath much more
> Establisht in safe unenvied Throne
> Yielded with full consent.

The sentence, "disentangled" (a rude but necessary procedure) and with all the syntactic ellipses filled in, goes something like this: "Though just right and the fixed laws of heaven did first create me [Satan] your leader, and next, your own free choice along with whatever else of merit hath been achieved by me in counsel or in fight . . ." all of that being the modifying subordinate clause, the main clause beginning with the word *yet*, in the sense of *still* . . . "still more has *this* loss [i. e., the loss of heaven] recovered at least thus far [i. e., to the extent that they find themselves still alive in hell and not utterly destroyed]— still more has this loss established me in a safe because an unenvied throne, yielded by all of you fallen angels in full consent." For who would want to be the most damned of all?

The inverted syntax of the pronoun *me* must first be clarified. The most obvious way is to pause, but, I think, to pause without letting the voice fall in pitch, or perhaps to allow the slightest sort of rise. The auditor needs to hold the pronoun in suspension until he hears the verb which governs it. Something like:

Me———— though just ri$^{ght}$....

The first two nouns of the dependent clause started by *though* form the beginning of a compound: both the heavenly *laws* and what is *right* created Satan leader ("right" in the sense of a moral as well as a legal sanction). So it is important to pronounce the expression *just right* in such a way as to avoid the implication of an adjectival phrase with *just* as modifying adverb, something dreadful like "Though I'm feeling just right," "in perfect spirits," or the like. The compound structure of noun subjects would perhaps be best indicated by intonating *just right* and *fixed laws of heaven* at a high pitch level, rising quickly above that of the surrounding words. This kind of intonational isolation and pointing conveys a sense of equal weight and parallelism, of correlative peaks above the dead level of the menial connecting words *though* and *and,* and the following predicate. Thus:

Me———— though just ri$^{ght}$ and the fixed laws of Heav$^{'n}$

The further parallelism of free choice can be secured by the same high-rising contour after the unchanged low-pitched, and somewhat hurried, predicate. Thus:

. . . though just ri$^{ght}$ and the fixed laws of Heav$^{'n}$

Did first create your Leader, next, free choi$^{ce,}$

And although the fourth noun component, *what besides hath been achieved of merit,* etc., is *structurally* subsidiary to the phrase *free choice,* it is logically parallel to the three preceding components. Four discrete things made Satan leader, and it is necessary to list them clearly, to give them equal vocal status. So the phrase *what besides hath been achieved,* etc., wants the high-rising pitch contour that has characterized the preceding three components, although its greater length needs a more rapid articulation to preserve the parallelism.

The final problem is to show orally that the rest of the sentence constitutes the main clause, the central assertion. A good way to achieve this is to give the subject—the phrase *this loss*—clear prominence and isolation by means of a very pronounced and complete rise-fall contour, a contour also clearly supported by the merely parenthetical status of the following modifying phrase. Something like the following:

> . . . yet this $^{l}o_{s_{s}}$
>
> Thus far at least recover'd, hath . . .

The word with the greatest degree of logical prominence in the sentence, and therefore the one which requires the clearest oral pointing, is *more.* The whole concession has been leading up to it: The word clinches the whole of Satan's claim to leadership, for the four qualifications of the initial dependent clause are, though persuasive in their own right, almost as nothing compared to the starkly convincing reality of the fall from heaven. Such a word needs the greatest accentual prominence in the sentence, in this case greater even than the prominence on *this loss.* It should rise higher and fall farther and perhaps have a slight pause after it:

> . . . yet this $^{l}o_{s_{s}}$
>
> Thus far at least recove$^{r'd}$, hath m$^{uch}$ $^{m}o_{r_{e}}$
> Establisht . . .

The rest of the sentence needs a low-pitched, though clear articulation, the better to set off the prominence of *more.* Thus, to summarize my suggested reading:

                                    fixed laws of Heav'n
Me        though    just right    and the
                                   free choice,
Did first create your Leader, next,
With what besides, in Counsel or in Fight,
Hath been achie v'd of merit,
                                   yet this loss
Thus far at least recover'd, hath much more
Establisht in safe unenvied Throne
Yielded with full consent.

Such a reading is solely to explicate, to illuminate the syntax. Try to imagine, to add in your mind's ear, all the other ingredients—of feeling, attitude, personality, identification, and so forth—necessary for a full and effective performance.

Let us turn to the interpreter's second task, that of identifying the speaker, the poem's *persona*. Remember the sorts of voice-particularizing features which we have already discussed: pitch range, vocal cord control, glottis control, pitch contour control, articulation control, rhythm control, resonance, and tempo. Assuming an interpreter with perfect command of these mechanisms—and he would be a gifted man indeed—his job is to select that combination of features which best represents the voice that he imagines the poem to suggest. (Notice that I say *poem* rather than *poet;* we cannot know what the poet intended except as that emerges from the poem itself.) With rare exceptions (for instance Hal Holbrook's very studied imitation of Mark Twain's voice) the identification expresses the interpreter's understanding, not the author's voice as actually heard or imagined. Since he does not have, and does not want, a specific model, what the interpreter seeks is not so much exactness as *plausibility,* or to use a forceful term from aesthetics, *verisimilitude.* What constitutes plausibility or verisimilitude will, of course, be determined by what he understands to be culturally typical of such a *persona:* an old, weary man; a man of intelligence and culture; a neurotic; or what have you. The interpreter's task, then, is very much like the painter's. The painter, even when reconstructing historical scenes, creates in terms of his own vision of how people look to him *at the moment.* If he is successful, his image achieves a kind of freedom from time, in deference to which the observer accepts the fact that the Virgin Mary happens to wear Renaissance costume or that Joseph looks very much like a North Italian peasant. These are conventions in which we participate in the interest of a vivid and larger human reality (unless our tastes have been so twisted by that specious historical realism cultivated in Hollywood that we are troubled by the minor anachronism). From the interpreter's point of view, too, historical realism is irrelevant; his business is with the living audience and what they consider to be convincing, and that is necessarily conditioned by what they hear around them every day.

The identificational cast of the voice is the ground, or base, upon which emotional effects are depicted. But I do not wish to give the impression of a hard and fast distinction between identificational and emotional features. There is a blurring of the edges by the very nature of life and growth. A man may have certain feelings so long and so persistently that they simply become a part of his character and find permanent, that is, identificational, manifestation in his voice. If a man has become melancholic—we think of Shakespeare's Jacques, for example—the sound of melancholy has come not merely to indicate his normal feeling of the moment, but to identify him. It is part of the very fiber of his personality, and not something superadded by temporary emotion. It is a very neat trick in interpretation and acting to convey passing feelings without canceling the impression of permanent attributes—say, for example, to render accurately the melancholic Jacques' moments of enthusiasm, for he certainly cannot sound enthusiastic in the same way that a naturally pleasant and happy person would be. But in many situations there is no contrast—the *persona* sounds like what he is, and whether he is like that permanently or only for the duration of the plot is not a serious literary question; it extends illegitimately beyond the bounds of the work of art, since there *is* only the duration of the plot. It is of the same order of fruitless speculation as, "How many children had Lady Macbeth?"

But emotions do sometimes change *within* a poem, as the extended example discussed in part II illustrates. Then it does make sense to note the distinction between identification and attitude. It is in this province of emotional expression that the interpreter has the greatest maneuverability. It is difficult for even the most versatile vocal manipulator to utterly change his voice quality; he will continue to sound something like his normal self simply because of the limits of his own vocal anatomy. But if he is at all competent, the depiction of emotions is a wide-open possibility. The emotions have typical phonological forms which are as conventional in some ways as are ordinary phonemes, those which form words, and are easily imitated. These forms, although occurring with individual variations, are known to the youngest and most naïve members of society —infants learn many of them before they learn language itself, and even intelligent animals, like dogs, can learn to distinguish angry from affectionate tones. We can all understand them in others and produce them ourselves, although some of us, actors by profession or temperament, are more proficient than others in manufacturing them at will, without really feeling the emotions they depict.

# II

Robert Browning's "The Bishop Orders His Tomb at St. Praxed's Church" is a dramatic monologue spoken by a dying ecclesiastic to his sons who are grouped around his deathbed. It is a study of an old man who either from illness or senility has difficulty controlling the wanderings of his mind. He utters the sententious pieties befitting his position, but these are made hypocritically hollow by what we learn of the way he has lived—he has conspired against one of his colleagues, has had a sinful relation with a woman, has stolen church property, and so forth. He longs for grace but is troubled by fear and suspicion that his sons will not provide the proper fittings for his burial. We cannot tell whether his fears are justified, but given the irregularity of the relationship and the treachery of the times, they probably are. A holy person, of course, is not supposed to worry about such things; he should rather be contemplating his removal to heaven. But the bishop is all too earthly. He is particularly concerned about the quality of the stone to be used for his tomb. He cannot make up his mind what sort he wants: basalt, antique black, jasper, or *lapis lazuli*. He is a great lapidophile, an addict of stone; he speaks of it in sensuous, loving terms, terms which might as easily refer to women or to food and wine or other sensual delights which, we may be sure, he has equally enjoyed in the past. But the bishop is an aesthete: his is not merely an appetite, but a genuine love and appreciation of beauty. His descriptions are as sensitive as an artist's: He revels in the silent seats of the choir, the airy dome where the angels and the lurking sunbeams live. He envisages a monument of luxurious style: a slab, nine columns, with the odd one at his feet, a frieze, a bas-relief, pans and nymphs, and so forth. These reveal the elegant taste of the Renaissance gentleman. And the indiscriminate mixture of paganism and Christianity is equally typical. Indeed, the bishop is as anomalous as his times, an era in which abstract piety lived side by side with fleshly hedonism without discomfort or even awareness of conflict. But he is a weak man, morally as well as physically. He is petty about status, and he takes a child's vindictive pleasure in imagining the discomfiture of his enemy, Gandolf, the former bishop of St. Praxed's church.

These, then, are some of the things an interpreter would find characteristic of the bishop and would attempt to articulate in his voice: his age, his ill health, his hypocritical piety, thinly covering a deep-seated sensuality, his suspicion of his sons and fear of their plans to deprive him of the monumental stone which he loves so gluttonously, and his petty vindictiveness. His age and ill health are identificational background characteristics against which the conflicting emotions play at appropriate moments through the poem.

The reader should follow the text as he listens closely to the relevant lines of the recorded performance by James Mason,[1] noting the way in which the bishop's voice and character have been illustrated. Although my purpose is primarily descriptive rather than evaluative, I find it difficult not to comment occasionally upon how a line is or might be read.

### THE BISHOP ORDERS HIS TOMB AT SAINT PRAXED'S CHURCH [2]

#### Rome, 15—

VANITY, said the preacher, vanity!
Draw round my bed: is Anselm keeping back?
Nephews—sons mine . . . ah God, I know not!
    Well—
She, men would have to be your mother once,
Old Gandolf envied me, so fair she was!        5
What's done is done, and she is dead beside,
Dead long ago, and I am Bishop since,
And as she died so must we die ourselves,

And thence ye may perceive the world's a dream.
Life, how and what is it? As here I lie
In this state-chamber, dying by degrees,
Hours and long hours in the dead night, I ask
"Do I live, am I dead?" Peace, peace seems all.
Saint Praxed's ever was the church for peace;
And so, about this tomb of mine. I fought    15
With tooth and nail to save my niche, ye know:
—Old Gandolf cozened me, despite my care;
Shrewd was that snatch from out the corner South
He graced his carrion with, God curse the same!
Yet still my niche is not so cramped but thence    20
One sees the pulpit o' the epistle-side,
And somewhat of the choir, those silent seats,
And up into the aery dome where live
The angels, and a sunbeam's sure to lurk:
And I shall fill my slab of basalt there,    25
And 'neath my tabernacle take my rest,
With those nine columns round me, two and two,
The odd one at my feet where Anselm stands:
Peach-blossom marble all, the rare, the ripe
As fresh-poured red wine of a mighty pulse.    30
—Old Gandolf with his paltry onion-stone,
Put me where I may look at him! True peach,
Rosy and flawless: how I earned the prize!
Draw close: that conflagration of my church
—What then? So much was saved if aught were    35
        missed!—
My sons, ye would not be my death? Go dig
The white-grape vineyard where the oil-press stood,
Drop water gently till the surface sink,
And if ye find . . . Ah God, I know not, I . . .
Bedded in store of rotten fig-leaves soft,    40
And corded up in a tight olive-frail,
Some lump, ah God, of *lapis lazuli*,
Big as a Jew's head cut off at the nape,
Blue as a vein o'er the Madonna's breast . . .

Sons, all have I bequeathed you, villas, all,      45
That brave Frascati villa with its bath,
So, let the blue lump poise between my knees,
Like God the Father's globe on both his hands
Ye worship in the Jesu Church so gay,
For Gandolf shall not choose but see and burst!      50
Swift as a weaver's shuttle fleet our years:
Man goeth to the grave, and where is he?
Did I say basalt for my slab, sons? Black—
'Twas ever antique-black I meant! How else
Shall ye contrast my frieze to come beneath?      55
The bas-relief in bronze ye promised me,
Those Pans and Nymphs ye wot of, and perchance
Some tripod, thyrsus, with a vase or so,
The Saviour at his sermon on the mount,
Saint Praxed in a glory, and one Pan      60
Ready to twitch the Nymph's last garment off,
And Moses with the tables . . . but I know
Ye mark me not! What do they whisper thee,
Child of my bowels, Anselm? Ah, ye hope
To revel down my villas while I gasp      65
Bricked o'er with beggar's mouldy travertine
Which Gandolf from his tomb-top chuckles at!
Nay, boys, ye love me—all of jasper, then!
'Tis jasper ye stand pledged to, lest I grieve
My bath must needs be left behind, alas!      70
One block, pure green as a pistachio-nut,
There's plenty jasper somewhere in the world—
And have I not Saint Praxed's ear to pray
Horses for ye, and brown Greek manuscripts,
And mistresses with great smooth marbly limbs?      75
—That's if ye carve my epitaph aright,
Choice Latin, picked phrase, Tully's every word,
No gaudy ware like Gandolf's second line—
Tully, my masters? Ulpian serves his need!
And then how I shall lie through centuries,      80
And hear the blessed mutter of the mass,

And see God made and eaten all day long,
And feel the steady candle-flame, and taste
Good strong thick stupefying incense-smoke!
For as I lie here, hours of the dead night,                85
Dying in state and by such slow degrees,
I fold my arms as if they clasped a crook,
And stretch my feet forth straight as stone can
     point,
And let the bedclothes, for a mortcloth, drop
Into great laps and folds of sculptor's-work:             90
And as yon tapers dwindle, and strange thoughts
Grow, with a certain humming in my ears,
About the life before I lived this life,
And this life too, popes, cardinals and priests,
Saint Praxed at his sermon on the mount,                  95
Your tall pale mother with her talking eyes,
And new-found agate urns as fresh as day,
And marble's language, Latin pure, discreet,
—Aha, ELUCESCEBAT quoth our friend?
No Tully, said I, Ulpian at the best!                    100
Evil and brief hath been my pilgrimage.
All *lapis*, all, sons! Else I give the Pope
My villas! Will ye ever eat my heart?
Ever your eyes were as a lizard's quick,
They glitter like your mother's for my soul,             105
Or ye would heighten my impoverished frieze,
Piece out its starved design, and fill my vase
With grapes, and add a vizor and a Term,
And to the tripod ye would tie a lynx
That in his struggle throws the thyrsus down,            110
To comfort me on my entablature
Whereon I am to lie till I must ask
"Do I live, am I dead?" There, leave me, there!
For ye have stabbed me with ingratitude
To death—ye wish it—God, ye wish it! Stone—             115
Gritstone, a-crumble! Clammy squares which sweat
As if the corpse they keep were oozing through—

And no more *lapis* to delight the world!
Well go! I bless ye. Fewer tapers there,
But in a row: and, going, turn your backs
—Ay, like departing altar-ministrants,
And leave me in my church, the church for peace,
That I may watch at leisure if he leers—
Old Gandolf—at me, from his onion-stone,
As still he envied me, so fair she was!  125

*Line 1.* The poem begins with a piety: the things of this
world are vain and worthless. How ironic it is that the
bishop should say this we soon learn from his expressed
and implied love of earthly beauties. The first word is
drawled out and given a great deal of breathiness, almost a
sigh, making the voice appropriately old and tired. Mason,
however, doesn't do as much as he might to make this hollow piety *sound* hollow. The voice is a little too animated
and too earnest; it should be more artificial. Perhaps Mason
felt that the bishop was a good enough actor to make such
*sententiae* appear reasonably sincere. Certainly he must
have been something of an actor to have carried on the way
he did all those years and still remain bishop. The trouble
with giving the word too much drawling and concentration
is that it makes it sound as if the bishop were really con-
demning his own life for its vanity. From later evidence, of
course, nothing seems further from the truth.

*Line 2.* Mason gives another strong identificational cue
to the speaker's age in line 2; on the name Anselm the voice
cracks slightly and weakens at a high intonational level.
The question itself is designed, I think, to hint at the fear
of disloyalty, which becomes clear, even obsessive, later in
the poem; but it is also perhaps to suggest the foolish
fondness of an unwisely partial parent for one child among
several, a child later referred to as "child of my bowels."
Mason very well conveys the foolishness and petulance of
the bishop-as-father.

*Line 3.* How should one interpret the third line? What

does "ah God, I know not" refer to? The bishop addresses
the group first as nephews and then as sons. If "ah God, I
know not" is connected with this address, then the implication is that there is no longer any need to dissemble—he is
about to die and nobody else but the sons are present anyway, and of course, *they* know who they are. So "ah God, I
know not" does not mean "I don't know whether you are
sons or nephews" but rather "I don't know whether to
bother keeping up the farce any longer that you are
nephews." The dots of ellipsis would then equal a colon,
although suggesting a longer pause. A good intonation
would be questioning rises on the words *sons* and *nephews,*
with a puzzled contour and sigh on "I know not." But Mason does not do this. He follows the rising, tentative
*nephews* with a *falling, affirmative* contour on *sons.* This
conveys another meaning. The affirmation is in no uncertain terms, and the initial catchy rise makes it sound
pleased, even a little sly, as if he were nudging the sons in
the ribs at the joke. Mason implies little or no connection
between "ah God, I know not" and the preceding address
to the sons. But what then can it refer to? I suppose something like *general* uncertainty might be Mason's reply—
"What is life?" "What am I doing here?" "Do I live or
die?" and so forth. This is possible, but, I feel, weaker than
the first interpretation. And in any case, if it were inten-
tional, there should have been a longer pause between the
two parts to effect a cleaner break. As it stands, it sounds
merely as if the interpreter, not the bishop, is indecisive
about the meaning. The last word in the line, *well,* however,
is suitably done; it is breathy, as of a man striving to catch
his breath, as old people do.

*Lines 4-5.* Lines 4 and 5 offer a slight problem in syntax-
clarification. Actually, unless we view the sentence as to-
tally broken off after *she* and begun anew—a very unsatis-
factory interpretation—it contains what a purist would call
a grammatical error. The syntax is inverted and elliptical

for something like "Old Gandolf envied me for having her"; it doesn't make much sense otherwise. *She,* then, the purist would say, must be in the wrong case: It should be the objective form *her* by the rule book, like Milton's form *me* in the passage discussed above. Browning succumbed to that tendency, common today, to use the case which corresponds to the syntactic territory in which the word finds itself. Just as most of us say "It is me" because the position after the verb is "objective territory," even though technically the nominative case is required, he wrote *she* because the word occurs in "subject territory." In any case, one has to clarify the inversion by strictly honoring the comma after *she* to avoid the ridiculous implication of *she-men.* Mason does this by rising considerably through *she* and handling *men* very gingerly, giving the /m/ phoneme a long drawl and rising through it too. One could bolster the effect in another way, namely, by pausing considerably after *she* and staying low on *men,* as in:

$$\text{Sh}^{\text{e}} \quad \text{men would have to be your }^{\text{mo}}\text{ther on}^{\text{ce}},$$

Another subtle and interesting clarificational problem—this one involving segmental phonology—occurs at the word *have.* This word, too, must be handled very gingerly, with great length and full voice and articulation given to the /v/, for weakening /v/ to /f/, as in /hæf/ /tɛ/ /biː/, spoken rapidly, would sound too much like the synonym for *must be.* Mason does not give it an adequately full treatment. One certainly wants to avoid the impression of "she-men who must be their mother"! Notice again the strong breathiness of *me* to show age. Mason successfully achieves a sound of admiring and loving wonder in the next half-line, chiefly by the slightly rising intonation and the soft, extremely breathy vocalization.

*Line 6.* The identification of age is achieved in a different way in the next line: the vocal cords are controlled in such a way as to sound gravelly and broken. The mood here is one of self-forgiveness (one can hardly imagine *this* bishop allowing his sins to eat him up; only greed and fear are able to do *that* to him). Mason strikes quite the right note, not at all heavy and just the slightest bit complacent, through the fall-rise on the second occurrence of the word *done.* The note of self-forgiveness is carried through to the second half of the line by the rise through *dead,* and again through *beside,* which seems to say, "She couldn't have suffered very much, so why blame me?"

*Line 7.* But as he says this, it also must occur to him that her absence does cause him pain. Mason quite correctly makes the phrase *Dead long ago* beginning the next line sound rueful, chiefly by pausing after *Dead* and rising high through *long* and falling through *ago.* The second half-line is read more noncommittally, to suit the matter-of-fact meaning. The bishop is neither proud nor humble about his position, probably secured as a family inheritance; he simply takes it as an occurrence—he lost her and then became bishop.

*Line 8.* As he talks in this reminiscent way, recalling how things have gone, it is natural that he should slip into another piety. Mason handles this one more appropriately than the first line, with just the right moralistic tone. The artificiality and detachment are conveyed by the intonation on the last two words: the word *die* rises, and so does *ourselves;* in fact, *ourselves* rises twice, with that peculiar insistence preachers use to call attention to a moral to be drawn.

*Line 9.* The bishop continues to moralize for a moment, his age and physical weakness being neatly touched upon again by the sloppy articulation of the $/\varepsilon/$ phoneme in *thence.*

*Lines 10-12.* But he soon returns to his own situation; notice how Mason cleverly weakens tone and voice quality as the bishop indulges in self-pity.

*Line 13.* Mason's very long pause between the two questions of line 13 strikes me as a little too portentous. It is to be noted that Browning only used a comma to separate them, and the second is virtually a repetition of the first, simply another way of asking the same thing. But Mason's interpretation of the next sentence, "Peace, peace seems all," is just right. The rapid shifts in intonation—down on the first *peace,* down and up on the second, up high on *seems,* and then starting low and going down on *all*— gives the whole a loving, caressing tone which perfectly communicates what we might assume to be the bishop's feelings about his rest to come.

*Lines 13-14.* Here there is a mixture of sensuality and womanly weakness, the tone of the last indulgence of a life-long self-indulger. We do not expect to hear anything of the moral athleticism of the truly devout, ready and eager for the rigors of the Judgment Day. Nothing, indeed, active at all; eternity is to be filled by a kind of passive lying around.

*Line 15.* But the bishop is the practical and canny businessman we would expect a Renaissance Italian bishop to be. He remembers the tone of affairs as he snaps out of his dreamy mood and takes up the business of the meeting, namely the architecture of his tomb. Mason marks the break by a sharp intake of breath, as if girding his vocal loins. The voice becomes more vigorous and vital as the bishop gets down to business; it is still breathy, as one would expect of a sick old man, but the heavy stress, the determined pitch-fall on *tomb* suggests that he has recaptured a little of his old power.

*Line 16.* Strong determination echoes through the next sentence, but Mason manages to convey that it is the false strength of a façade, not of a whole true building. This is brilliantly achieved by weakening the articulation of the word *niche* so that it is sloppy and uncontrolled, the way a drunkard would speak, or an old man who is trying to sound resolute, but whose muscle tone is gone. And the old-timer's colloquialism "y'know" is also well done. The whole effect is of a man who has lost his power to compel attention and yet tries, rather pitifully, to be assertive. But all is too shaky. The effort is too much and he has to swallow to recover his strength. Can you hear the swallow?

*Lines 17-19.* Mason might be accused of being a little too subtle, of trying to achieve too many effects in the next three lines, but I think he's justified, and I find I like the performance very much. Obviously he feels that the bishop can both curse Gandolf and admire him at the same time, or at least admire his wiliness, for there is a slight but telling bit of whimsy in the expression. *Cozened* sounds earnest enough, with a high-rising contour, but that it is a mock earnestness (or, better, a half-earnestness, for, after all, the bishop *does* care) becomes apparent from the performance of the next line. *Shrewd* is said with grudging admiration, conveyed by the sound of a smile. (A smile *does* make a sound, of course, namely the effect on the segmental phonemes of curling the lips upward, and also the brighter tone of the voice which results from getting the lips up and out of the way of the resonating breath stream.) And the rendition of the word *out* is worth careful attention—it has the slightest bit of extra aspiration in it, suggesting a barely suppressed laugh. "God curse the same" is said with a low and steady intonation which suggests not so much deadly hatred as a kind of *pro forma* imprecation: the bishop sounds as if he has been cursing Gandolf for so many years that he does it now more out of habit than out of real feeling.

*Lines 20-24.* The next several lines are brighter, as the bishop finds that his spot isn't so bad after all; his love of beauty is aroused by the vista from his tomb, as he naïvely assumes that he's going to have eyes to see it after death. Hell, apparently, is no possibility to him. Mason achieves a cheerful, engaging, sprightly, even cozy tone to match the cozy future life the bishop imagines for himself, mostly by a high-pitch contour, made a little ridiculous by the wizened squeezing of the voice. Here, at the moment of the bishop's most naïve vanity, Mason makes him sound most senile and doddering.

*Lines 25-28.* The cozy, almost namby-pamby quality continues, chiefly through the up-and-down "just-so" intonation, like a child arranging her dolls in just a certain order.

*Lines 29-30.* The discussion of his tomb stimulates the bishop's chief passion, his love of stone. He thinks of marble first, for the columns. For this, the bishop's last great lust, Mason senses the need to make the descriptions sound truly lustful. He literally has the bishop drooling, filling his mouth with extra saliva. The liquid consonants like /l/ and even the stops like /p/ sound positively juicy.

*Line 31.* Midway in this orgiastic celebration of stone, a moody vindictiveness descends upon the bishop as he gloats over Gandolf's imagined envy. Mason shows its parentheticalness by starting at a very low pitch and rising only slightly. By means of curt articulation and choppy rising intonation contours he conveys the contemptuous note very well.

*Line 32.* The vindictive triumph of the next line is clearly communicated by a long *descending* intonation contour, again with slightly spread lips, but this time suggesting a sneer more than a chuckle, although a sneer softened by the childishness of age.

*Lines 32-33.* And then the ecstasy of stone is resumed.

*Lines 33-35.* The bishop now proceeds to reveal a dark secret: he has stolen and hidden a piece of church property, a lump of *lapis lazuli*. Mason's tones are appropriately conspiratorial. The volume drops and the lips come closer together so that the segmental phonemes are "cloaked" and "darkened." As the bishop begins to give instructions to his sons about how to recover the long-concealed piece of stone, we get a second and stronger hint that he suspects their faithlessness. There is a long pause, and he addresses them in a very tentative, questioning way, a suspicious half-rise through the word *sons*.

*Line 36.* And then the question "ye would not be my death" is spoken with no final rise at all; from the performance alone one could not detect that it is a question rather than a statement. I think Mason gives it this dead-level quality to convey the note of uncertainty—the bishop doesn't really know whether he's asking or telling them; indeed, he may feel some fear about asking them because they might say yes. It's very much like a mother saying apprehensively to a rebellious little boy, "You're going to be good now, aren't you, Tommy?"

*Lines 36-46.* As he gives directions for the recovery of the beloved, precious stone, the bishop's voice becomes more and more excited. The excitement is conveyed by increased tempo and a greater degree of trembling and voice tremulo, and pitch rising ever higher and higher until the climax. Midway the bishop has to stop twice to control himself, ironically appealing to the God who has surely condemned him by now. Mason punctuates the oath with sharp intakes of breath.

*Lines 47-49.* At the height of the bishop's fantasy, the stone imagined poised, almost sexually, between his legs—stone *is* this old man's sex—Mason catches the sensual tone that we've heard before, with its juicy labials and liquids and long, soaring, and eloquent contours. The sound of excitement continues, but now the excitement of elation rather than conspiracy.

*Line 50.* And, of course, the climax of his pleasure is to imagine Gandolf exploding with envy. The word *burst* is said with the brightest of timbres, as the lips are curled back and away from the emerging sounds—the bishop's envy is the most animated thing left to him, and it is conveyed in brassy and ebullient tones.

*Lines 51-54.* Suddenly another one of those well-worn pieties that are never very far away drops from the bishop's lips. What prompts it? A sudden pain? Some twinge of guilt about the orgy of petulance and greed just expressed? Some sense of the need to calm down? We can't tell from the poem, and the cause is not as important, anyhow, as the effect. It is one more rapid and complete shift of mood in the man's wandering mind. Mason punctuates with a double sigh, and continues sighing through the piety. The tempo is slow and the voice grave. The shifts of mood are becoming more rapid and more extreme, for at the same moment that the moralism occurs to him, his fancy suddenly and anxiously changes its lapidary preference, something which is to happen twice more. Did he say basalt? He meant another kind of stone, antique black. Mason doesn't get quite enough weakness and anxiety into this line for my taste. It isn't simply a question, but a symptom of the dying man's growing incapacity to control his thoughts, mixed with the growing fear of betrayal after death.

*Lines 54-56.* The voice becomes animated and happy again as he contemplates the visual effects of the ornament upon his tomb.

*Line 57.* And at the mention of those amorous demibeings, the pans and nymphs, Mason makes the voice gleeful, almost ribald with lustfulness; but it is an old man's rather detached lustfulness, the lustfulness of the spectator rather than the performer. The pronunciation of *Pans* conveys the correct pitch of excitement and voyeuristic pleasure by means of an explosive articulation and rapid and complete fall in pitch.

*Lines 57-62.* The jumble of sacred and profane images with which the bishop wants to adorn his tomb forms the clearest and most concentrated expression of the bewildering mixture of piety and hedonism that inform his character. They appear in a simple and indiscriminate list: "Moses with the tables," for example, gets left in the air by ellipsis dots; he is an afterthought. Duty requires the presence of the worthies, the Saviour, Moses, and St. Praxed, but one's sensual and aesthetic enthusiasms are all for pagan antiquity. Mason handles this well by vacillating between tones he has already established elsewhere as, respectively, sensual and pious.

*Lines 60-61.* Bawdy Pan undressing a nymph is described in the fond and caressing way that one might use of a favorite toy or pet. The focus is at the word *garment,* and loving fondness is conveyed by giving a slight initial rising onset to the predominantly falling contour of that word.

*Line 62.* "And Moses with the tables" is appropriately left hanging in midair, the tone neither falling nor rising.

*Lines 62-63.* But in the midst of his pleasure, the bishop notices or imagines he notices, the sons whispering. This touches off the hostility, bred of fear, that has been brewing under the surface since the beginning of the poem. It is the first time that we hear pure anger; it is conveyed by harsh voice quality, sharp increase in loudness, and forceful articulation.

*Lines 63-64.* Then, as the bishop asks Anselm what they're whispering about, Mason switches to a conspiratorial tone, in the same way as before, but this time with the addition of definite whisper in the last part of the sentence.

*Line 64-67.* Mason starts out the sentence with the same sort of tone, but shifts, interestingly, about halfway through, into a kind of whining complaint; for, of course, the bishop is quite impotent to take action, by condition, now, if not by temperament. It's not quite clear how Mason manages this—there is a gradual rise in intonation and loudness, but that serves merely to show increased excitement. There may be something about the intonation of the word *travertine* that contributes to this effect—a delayed rise on the last syllable combined with a squeezing of the voice that sounds like a suppressed sob.

*Lines 68-69.* The bishop then pleads with his sons to build his tomb out of jasper, the stone which was used to construct his bath. The pleading or wheedling tone with a slight admixture of petulance is chiefly conveyed by over-high pitch and a sudden sharp dip on the crucial word, *jasper.* Mason has the bishop say "Nay, boys, ye love me" rapidly and with an uncertain contour, neither question nor assertion but something in between, and hurries him on to the next sentence without giving them a chance to answer, again as if he feared they might really speak the truth.

*Lines 69-71.* The clause after the word *lest* is said in lamenting tones, as if the bishop really could project his feelings the other side of death and know how he would feel—deprived, like an Egyptian pharaoh or a Viking king who has been buried without all his rightful property. The lines in which the block of jasper is described are phonetically juicy in the same way that we have heard before, with an added bit of voice huskiness to make the sensuality even stronger.

*Lines 72-75.* The bishop tries to bribe them; he will intervene with his patron saint if they get his epitaph right, and they will be rewarded with the kinds of things that he himself has loved so well: horses, manuscripts, and women. The offer is supported by rising parallel pitch contours, clearly symbolic here, of wheedling.

*Line 76.* Having allowed the hook to settle, the bishop yanks the string to insure the catch. Mason understands and respects Browning's punctuation—the dash before "That's" in line 76, which helps to set the bargain in clear terms—by giving triumphant accent to "That's" (he might equally have done it on the next word, "if"). This accent is achieved by considerable loudness and high isolating pitch and beginning the next word at a low pitch with clear-cut, glottal-stop onset.

*Line* 77. An important bit of syntax-clarification is needed in the next line. The bishop wants his epitaph to consist of quotations from Tully, that is, Cicero; however, obviously, the meaning is not "every word that Cicero wrote" (no tombstone would be large enough to carry all that), but rather "every one of the words on the tombstone should come from Cicero." To insure this meaning it is essential to have a decisive pause between "Tully's" and "every," to keep the appositional status of "every word" absolutely clear. Mason doesn't pause long enough to my taste, although the separate pitch contour on the phrase *every word* may be enough for most listeners to keep the structures separate. The only truly disastrous thing would be to use only one pitch contour, to read

Tully's every w$_{\text{ord}}$

or the like. As the bishop expresses his literary preferences, we get a taste of the other, less sensual side of his hedonism. Mason conveys this by an exacting and elegant preciseness of speech, with none of the saliva produced for the other mood. The bishop's pleasure here is entirely cerebral.

*Lines* 78-79. But not far away is the pleasure of feeling contemptuous, this time about Gandolf's poor taste in Latin. Did Gandolf know enough to request Cicero? Hardly; Ulpian, that hack, was good enough for him! Listen to how the contempt in the sentence "Ulpian serves his need" is conveyed: by low, level intonation, compressed vocal cavity with tight lips and curt rapid tempo, as of speaking of something distasteful to get it over in a hurry.

*Lines* 80-84. In the next four lines, sensualism mixes with contentment and peace as the bishop dreams again of his future life. Mason draws the lines out slowly and lov-

ingly; these are the things that the bishop knows and treas-
ures—mass, communion, candles, and incense—and they
are the things with which he fills his mind to avoid thinking
about the horrors of death and filial ingratitude. The phrase
*God made* is conveyed particularly effectively by a double
precipitous fall and a tender voice quality. Later, the image becomes more and more sensual, and saliva once again
begins to flow.

*Lines 85-90.* In the next ten lines, the bishop celebrates
his death in stately, slow, and formal terms. He is dying in
state, hardening into death like a stone statue; he arranges
his limbs in the stiff, bedraped funereal style so commonly
found on tombs in the great cathedrals of Europe. He fits
himself into the visual effect which his imagination has already created. The tone throughout is appropriately weak,
slow, dying, passive, formal. The timbre is soft and muf-
fled, like the drums beaten at Renaissance funerals. And
since the bishop pictures such a rosy future for himself, it
is appropriate that he should enjoy the tableau, and the note
of pleasure creeps familiarly into the dying formalism.

*Lines 91-95.* As he indulges himself, the bishop's voice
resumes that soft, passive, womanly note heard before. But
it shifts as the kaleidoscope of visions shifts from one figure
to the next.

*Line 96.* As the first four lines get weaker and weaker,
more and more pious and beatific, suddenly the voice firms,
becomes robust and sexy, as he remembers his mistress. A
smile appears in the voice again at the word *eyes,* a reminiscent, affectionate grin, almost, but not quite, a leer.

*Lines 97-98.* It is inevitable that the other grand passions
of his life—stone and Latin—should stray back into his
mind at precisely this moment.

*Lines 99-100.* Round and round whirl his thoughts.
Latin calls up Cicero and how the bishop misled Gandolf
into thinking Ulpian the better prose master. Gandolf
had said, "But Cicero was distinguished . . . Elucesce-

bat . . . ," to which the wily bishop responded, "No, Don't use Tully, for Ulpian had the best style." And here, as always, vindictiveness arouses vocal vigor. Listen to the canny reading of the clause "Ulpian at the best." The sentence starts out as if the accent on the name *Ulpian* were specially emphatic. But there is a second rise and fall on *best* which makes the sentence sound patronizing: the bishop not only assured Gandolf that he knew best about literary style, but he also knew that his victim would follow his recommendation implicitly. No wonder the bishop is afraid of the duplicity of his sons, for it is likely that they take after their father.

*Lines 101-102.* Toss in another piety, which, of course, has nothing to do with guilt but functions as a time filler and respite, and on comes another burst of greed and fear. I don't know what the relative values of these stones were in the bishop's day, but it looks as if they are meant to build up to a climax of preciousness. The excitement in Mason's voice breaks in upon the dead hollowness of the preceding piety like reality breaking in upon fantasy.

*Line 102.* The petulance of the threat—to give the Pope his villas if they don't promise—is conveyed chiefly by the intonation, a steep rise to *Pope* and then down, and level to the end of the sentence.

*Line 103.* The tone of the question is irritated, hurt, and impatient; it is conveyed by that compression and narrowing of the intonational range, discussed above, that strikes English ears as distinctly unpleasant.

*Lines 104-105.* Mason achieves a very unusual tonal balance in the next lines. The bishop continues to be angry and fearful, but he cannot help feeling a certain admiration for the power of his sons and their mother. The admiration is conveyed by bright metallic timbre and a kind of awed lengthening of the word *lizard's.*

*Line 106.* But then he thinks of what else they can do to ruin the effect of his tomb, and his voice becomes excitedly petulant and childish in complaint. Listen to the quavering of the voice on the word *frieze.*

*Lines 107-110.* Petulance is also clearly indicated by the distinctive early fall and low sustention in the words *Term* and *down* in the second and fourth of these lines.

*Lines 111-113.* The final part of the sentence, a kind of afterthought, is made ironic and detached in Mason's rendition. The tone that follows is more breathy than ever, an exhausted half-whisper. The depth of the bishop's despair and exhaustion cannot now be merely the product of distrust and fear. By this time it is the horror and uncertainty of death itself that is depressing him.

*Lines 113-115.* And now the masks are off and the masquerade over. The bishop has a moment of complete contact with reality; not only are the sons recognized for what they are, but he also acknowledges his powerlessness to do anything to change their nefarious plans. Mason's tone becomes admirably dry and emotionless or just the least bit disgusted.

*Line 115.* And then, in one of the sincerest and most direct utterances of the poem, the full measure of the bishop's hatred is communicated by a very low-level pitch contour and growling voice quality.

*Lines 116-118.* The wheel turns again and the bishop falls into a fearful revery about the corruption awaiting him; the horror of death finds its symbol in stone, too, but in wretched, spongy stone, grit-stone, whose porosity cannot keep the body in. The revery is appropriately delivered, first in tones that convey disgust (by means of extremely low pitch and a spitting out of the consonants). Then the voice rises, and disgust gets mixed with a kind of resigned horror. And finally, it sinks to a half-whisper, as the consequences of death—the disappearance of beautiful, sensual objects, like *lapis lazuli*—dawns upon the bishop.

*Lines 119-121.* Again the bishop momentarily recovers his sense of reality; in calm, dry tones he instructs the sons to leave him. He even masters a professional, conventional blessing, and is struck by the visual effect of their departure.

*Line 122.* The bishop asks to be left in his church, the church for peace; but after the anguish he has just been through, how hollow and mocking that phrase must seem to him. Mason catches just the right effect by delaying, by pausing abruptly between *for* and *peace,* as if he started out with a pat phrase and discovered halfway through how dismally ironic and far from the truth it was.

*Lines 123-125.* And once again his mind shifts to that which seems to give him most comfort in his dying moments, Gandolf's envy. For this climax of vindictiveness Mason's voice sounds positively gloating. It lightens and rises as he smiles, even chuckles at Gandolf's discomfiture. And in his final words, remembering the beauteous woman he loved, the tone switches again, suddenly, but convincingly, to complete adoration.


A colleague of mine, a professor of literature sensitive to the spoken word, once remarked that in general he disliked hearing professional actors interpret poetry. His reason was that they tend to put too much stock in local effects, what he called, if I remember, "dramatic bits." It was as if, he felt, they were so anxious to extract every drop of juice from the part (they *would* think of the depiction of the *persona* as a "part") that they lost sight of the other interpretational responsibilities, like keeping the meter and related sound effects, that is, conveying those aspects of poetry which distinguish it from drama. I recall agreeing with him, at least insofar as lyric poetry was concerned. But it strikes me that a poem like Browning's "The Bishop Orders His Tomb" positively needs the "local-effect–dramatic-bit" orientation, not merely because it is in a mixed genre, dramatic monologue, but because of the peculiar nature of the bishop's character. As we have seen, his mind is caught in a vicious and rapidly rotating circle; he's on one of those emotional merry-go-rounds that sick people often ride. And so it is not only ornamentally appropriate, but functionally necessary for Mason to be sensitive to every shift in mood, every slight changing nuance of feeling. Regardless of the general validity of my colleague's remark (and I still think it carries an element of truth), it is clear that a performance like Mason's is a highly effective interpretation of the poem.

One needs to make close line-by-line examinations to sense fully the subtleties of interpretation; the articulation of a poem can be meaningful only with closest reference to its full meaning. The efforts may seem arduous and clumsy, but the results will be very helpful to the neophyte interpreter. In these efforts, the study of linguistics may help him specify and describe the clarificational, identificational, and emotional functions of oral interpretation.

NOTES

1. Caedmon Record TC 1048 (1956). All references to James Mason's interpretation of "The Bishop Orders His Tomb" refer to this recording.
2. The text of the poem follows the one reprinted by Caedmon and issued with the recording.

RECOMMENDED READING

A good general introduction to linguistic methodology is H. A. Gleason, *An Introduction to Descriptive Linguistics* (New York: Holt, Rinehart, and Winston, 1961).

The terms for paralinguistic effects come from George L. Trager, "Paralanguage: A First Approximation," *Studies in Linguistics,* XIII (1958), 1-12.

The three systems which have been devised to describe American English intonation are Kenneth Pike, *The Intonation of American English* (Ann Arbor: University of Michigan Press, 1945); George L. Trager and Henry Lee Smith, Jr., *An Outline of English Structure* (Norman, Okla.: Battenberg Press, 1951; Washington: ACLS, 1956); and articles by Dwight Bolinger, particularly "A Theory of Pitch Accent in English," *Word,* XIV (1958), 109-149.

For the emotional implications of intonation, see Elisabeth Uldall, "Attitudinal Meanings Conveyed by Intonation Contours," *Language and Speech,* III (1960), 223-234, and Ivan Fonagy and Klara Magdics, "Emotional Patterns in Intonation and Music," *Zeitschrift für Phonetik Sprachwissenschaft und Kommunikationsforschung,* XVI (1963), 293-326.

The passage from Milton's *Paradise Lost* is further discussed in Seymour Chatman, "Linguistics and Teaching Introductory Literature," *Readings in Applied English Linguistics,* ed. Harold B. Allen, 2nd ed. (New York: Appleton-Century-Crofts, 1964), pp. 500-506.

## Projects

It is very profitable to *compare* various recordings of readings of the same poem. The differences dramatize the importance of the interpreter who amplifies or diminishes, adds or subtracts, communicates or confuses, enriches or impoverishes the poem's meaning. For the recordings listed below, attempt a line-by-line analysis of the sort presented in this chapter and come to some conclusions about the comparative excellence of the performances or about the specific vocal characteristics which serve clarificational, identificational, or emotional functions.

1. Compare Cyril Cusack's recording of "The Leaden Echo and the Golden Echo" ("The Poetry of Gerard Manley Hopkins," Caedmon TC 1111) with Robert Speaight's recording of the same poem ("The Poems of William Blake and Gerard Manley Hopkins," Spoken Arts 814). What similar qualities do the two readers use to distinguish between the "leaden echo" and the "golden echo"? Which *persona* seems to be soliloquizing; which seems to be speaking to an audience?

2. On the same two recordings referred to in question 1, compare Cusack's and Speaight's readings of "The Windhover." Which *persona* seems older? What intonational qualities convey the impression of age?

3. Compare Speaight's reading of "The Lamb" and "The Tiger" with Sir Ralph Richardson's reading of these two poems ("The Poetry of Blake," Caedmon TC 1101). Through what means does Richardson manage to achieve a greater contrast between "The Lamb" and "The Tiger" than Speaight does? Pay particular attention to Richardson's *rate*. Does it seem more appropriate for the poems than Speaight's? What other qualities besides rate enable Richardson to convey clearly the emotions of the speaker of "The Tiger"?

4. Compare Dame Sybil Thorndike's reading of "Tears, Idle Tears" ("Poetry of Tennyson," Caedmon TC 1080) with Eric Portman's ("Palgrave's Golden Treasury," Caedmon TC 2011). Contrast the emotions of the two *personae*. How are these different emotions conveyed? Which reader conveys a better sense of rhythm? Which reader communicates a climactic structure? Does the poem itself reach a climax? Note the differences in the readings of these lines, especially the handling of the pronoun "one":

> Sad as the last which reddens over one
> That sinks with all we love below the verge

Which reader does the better job of "syntax clarification"?

5. Compare Theodore Marcuse's reading of "To a Skylark" ("Keats and Shelley," Lexington 7505) with Claire Bloom's ("Palgrave's Golden Treasury," Caedmon TC 2011). Which reader does the better job of "syntax clarification"? Would you agree or disagree with this statement: Marcuse's exploitation of local effects merely calls attention to his own vocal efforts?

# PART II

## The Extrinsic Approach

# CHAPTER FOUR

# RHETORICAL ANALYSIS:

## Persuasive Strategies
## in the Structure of
## John Donne's "Satire III"

*THOMAS O. SLOAN*

## I

Rhetoric is the faculty of discovering in any situation the available means of persuasion; as a discipline, it is a practical art, whose principles are most easily discernible in the literary genres of speech and essay. Poetics, or poetry, is a fine art, a discipline that studies the structuring of imaginative discourse, primarily in the literary genres of lyric, narrative, and drama. The central difference between the two in any literary creative process is that rhetoric is a *faculty,* an ability to effect persuasion, requiring subtle knowledge of the psychology of audiences and of communicative strategies, whereas poetics is a body of knowledge concerned with aesthetic literary *structures,* with the putting together of discourse in such a way that the work gives pleasure to its readers or hearers. Rhetoric in discourse and poetry in discourse are esteemed and evaluated for different reasons: rhetoric, as in the speech or the essay, for the writer's effectiveness in teaching or persuading his audience; poetry, as in the lyric, narrative, or drama, for artistry of structure and effectiveness as a potential cause of pleasurable experience. To study a discourse rhetorically requires studying it in terms of its social environment, especially in terms of its audience. To study a discourse poetically requires studying the completeness of its structure, that feeling of "wholeness" described in Chapter Two.

Over three hundred years ago, John Donne said in one of his sermons as Dean of St. Paul's Cathedral that "Rhetoric will make absent and remote things present to your understanding. . . . Poetry is a counterfeit Creation, and makes things that are not, as though they were." The distinction is no more complex than the one we have already made. Rhetoric is a faculty that is most obvious in discourse which addresses itself directly to the understanding of an audience, usually on specific, practical, temporal issues within an existing social situation—as speeches and essays usually do. The art of poetry is best seen in that discourse which creates its own world, which provides a structuring of experience, both of which (the structure and the experience) the poet finds in his imagination—as is usually the case with lyrics, narratives, and dramas. Poetry finds its elements, some, many, or all, in the world of imagination; rhetoric belongs to a different world, the world of everyday reality, where the imagination stands in the presence of other people. But these are all extreme distinctions; rhetoric is a faculty whose operation we may admire in a poetical discourse, and poetry is an art whose creative force may enhance the effectiveness of a rhetorical discourse.

But many critics in our time seem determined rigorously to maintain these distinctions and to apply them in practical criticism in such a way as to do harm to the stature of rhetoric. John Donne made his distinctions at a time when training in rhetoric was central to the education of a poet or of a reader of poetry, a time when the two arts would be distinguished no more than one might attempt to draw a distinction between the legs of a compass: the distinction might be drawn, but with the tacit understanding that the two are useful mostly because they are or can be joined. It was a time when, looked at from certain modern perspectives, the arts were utterly confused, when critics were too bewildered by rhetoric ever fully to comprehend the nature of poetry.

Certainly some distinction is necessary. It has been demonstrated that many poems in the premodern period (before our attempts in literary criticism rigorously to exclude rhetorical considerations from our appreciation of poetry) were misread and misjudged because they were approached primarily through rhetorical avenues. However, it is also true that now we stand in almost the opposite danger, of misreading and misjudging poems by our exclusion of all rhetorical considerations. R. S. Crane has presented a brilliantly articulated critical program, based on Aristotelian principles, for the examination of literature on literary grounds, "poetry *qua* poetry." "The Aristotelian expert in poetics," Crane states, ". . . must know a good many different things besides poetry, but it is equally true that he becomes an expert in poetics by virtue precisely of his ability to subordinate the terms and premises he derives from metaphysics, physics, ethics, politics, rhetoric, psychology, and so on, to the peculiar principles of his own science." [1] The critic using the rhetorical analysis in an attempt to *supplant* the principles of poetics in the analysis and evaluation of poems is no less wise than the modern expert in poetics who ignores any help, advice, or direction that rhetoric may provide. We stand in the biggest danger of misreading literary works like John Donne's "Satire III," a poem that is as much rhetorical as it is poetical, a poem whose nature cannot be experienced by the critic who refuses to look beyond the spectrum of "pure poetry."

## II

Of all the Renaissance poets, John Donne is one of the most highly esteemed by modern critics and poets. His poems were among the first to receive modern critical treatment by means of the dramatic analysis. His love lyrics lend themselves well to evaluation by such qualities as "multivalence," "ambiguity," "irony," "complexity of attitudes," or whatever quality is most critically prized. But the following poem is not a love lyric; it is, rather, a satire, a poem designed to hold public vices up for scorn. The dramatic analysis when based only upon an *intrinsic* study of the text of the poem will take us only part of the way into its meaning, for the structure of this poem is "open-ended." That is, even to be understood, this poem must be read in terms of its social environment. The structure of this poem depends upon certain features that are not contained within the poem itself. We shall find those features best by analyzing the operation of the rhetorical faculty in this poem.

One critic employing the dramatic analysis intrinsically has analyzed this poem as a soliloquy, thoughts uttered in meditative isolation. According to this critic, the speaker of this poem reasons himself through a series of alternatives and finally arrives at a concept of truth that will allow his will to act.[2] Try reading the poem aloud as a soliloquy. What sort of person seems to be speaking these thoughts to himself?

### SATIRE III
Kind pity chokes my spleen; brave scorn forbids
Those tears to issue which swell my eye-lids;
I must not laugh, nor weep sins, and be wise,
Can railing then cure these worn maladies?
Is not our Mistress fair Religion,                    5
As worthy of all our Soul's devotion,

As virtue was to the first blinded age?
Are not heaven's joys as valiant to assuage
Lusts, as earth's honor was to them? Alas,
As we do them in means, shall they surpass     10
Us in the end, and shall thy father's spirit
Meet blind Philosophers in heaven, whose merit
Of strict life may be imputed faith, and hear
Thee, whom he taught so easy ways and near
To follow, damn'd? O if thou dar'st, fear this;     15
This fear great courage, and high valor is.
Dar'st thou aid mutinous Dutch, and dar'st thou lay
Thee in ships' wooden Sepulchers, a prey
To leaders' rage, to storms, to shot, to dearth?
Dar'st thou dive seas, and dungeons of the earth?     20
Hast thou courageous fires to thaw the ice
Of frozen North discoveries? and thrice
Colder than Salamanders, like divine
Children in th'oven, fire of Spain, and the line,
Whose countries limbecks to our bodies be,     25
Canst thou for gain bear? and must every he
Which cries not, Goddess, to thy Mistress, draw,
Or eat thy poisonous words? courage of straw!
O desperate coward, wilt thou seem bold, and
To thy foes and his (who made thee to stand     30
Sentinell in his world's garrison) thus yield,
And for forbidden wars, leave th'appointed field?
Know thy foes: The foul Devil (whom thou
Strivest to please,) for hate, not love, would allow
Thee fain, his whole Realm to be quit; and as     35
The world's all parts wither away and pass,
So the world's self, thy other lov'd foe, is
In her decrepit wane, and thou loving this,
Dost love a withered and worn strumpet; last,
Flesh (itself's death) and joys which flesh can taste,     40
Thou lovest; and thy fair goodly soul, which doth
Give this flesh power to taste joy, thou dost loathe.
Seek true religion. O where? Mirreus

Thinking her unhous'd here, and fled from us,
Seeks her at Rome; there, because he doth know          45
That she was there a thousand years ago,
He loves her rags so, as we here obey
The statecloth where the Prince sat yesterday.
Crantz to such brave Loves will not be inthrall'd,
But loves her only, who at Geneva is call'd          50
Religion, plain, simple, sullen, young,
Contemptuous, yet unhandsome; As among
Lecherous humors, there is one that judges
No wenches wholesome, but coarse country drudges.
Graius stays still at home here, and because          55
Some Preachers, vile ambitious bawds, and laws
Still new like fashions, bid him think that she
Which dwells with us, is only perfect, he
Embraceth her, whom his Godfathers will
Tender to him, being tender, as Wards still          60
Take such wives as their Guardians offer, or
Pay values. Careless Phrygius doth abhor
All, because all cannot be good, as one
Knowing some women whores, dares marry none.
Graccus loves all as one, and thinks that so          65
As women do in divers countries go
In divers habits, yet are still one kind,
So doth, so is Religion; and this blind-
ness too much light breeds; but unmoved thou
Of force must one, and forc'd but one allow;          70
And the right; ask thy father which is she,
Let him ask his; though truth and falsehood be
Near twins, yet truth a little elder is;
Be busy to seek her, believe me this,
He's not of none, nor worst, that seeks the best.          75
To adore, or scorn an image, or protest,
May all be bad; doubt wisely; in strange way
To stand inquiring right, is not to stray;
To sleep, or run wrong, is. On a huge hill,
Cragged, and steep, Truth stands, and he that will          80

Reach her, about must, and about must go;
And what the hill's suddenness resists, win so;
Yet strive so, that before age, death's twilight,
Thy Soul rest, for none can work in that night.
To will, implies delay, therefore now do:                    85
Hard deeds, the body's pains; hard knowledge too
The mind's endeavors reach, and mysteries
Are like the Sun, dazzling, yet plain to all eyes.
Keep the truth which thou hast found; men do not
    stand
In so ill case here, that God hath with his hand      90
Sign'd Kings blank-charters to kill whom they hate,
Nor are they Vicars, but hangmen to Fate.
Fool and wretch, wilt thou let thy Soul be tied
To man's laws, by which she shall not be tried
At the last day? Oh, will it then boot thee         95
To say a Philip, or a Gregory,
A Harry, or a Martin taught thee this?
Is not this excuse for mere contraries,
Equally strong? cannot both sides say so?
That thou mayest rightly obey power, her bounds
    know;                                            100
Those passed, her nature, and name is chang'd; to
    be
Then humble to her is idolatry.
As streams are, Power is; those blest flowers that
    dwell
At the rough stream's calm head, thrive and do
    well,
But having left their roots, and themselves given    105
To the stream's tyrannous rage, alas, are driven
Through mills, and rocks, and woods, and at last,
    almost
Consum'd in going, in the sea are lost:
So perish Souls, which more choose men's unjust
Power from God claim'd, than God himself to
    trust.[3]                                         110

"Satire III" is one of Donne's five satires, all written during the closing decade of the sixteenth century, when Donne was in his early twenties. As noted earlier, one critic has analyzed this poem as a soliloquy, claiming that all five satires are spoken by the same *persona*. According to this critic, the *persona* is a retiring scholar living in London, one who is occasionally persuaded to leave his study and wander through the city and who vents his wrath on evidences of encroaching materialism. Certainly "Satire I" is spoken by such a *persona,* and in all five poems the speaker lashes out at the degeneration of values in sixteenth-century London.

However, if this poem is a soliloquy spoken by a retiring scholar, it suffers from a lack of dramatic appropriateness. All the images of adventure and fighting (especially in lines 15-43) would hardly be used by a retiring scholar to reason with himself. Furthermore, any poem called a "satire" always has a public purpose. If this satire is in the form of a soliloquy, surely it was designed to teach or persuade people who would overhear these uttered thoughts. For example, if we were to suppose this soliloquy is an internal monologue ostensibly delivered by a man's conscience berating his own lustfulness and ambitiousness, we need to view the subtle strategies whereby the portrait of that lust and ambition pricks the conscience of the poem's *real* audience (as if the emphasis were "Dar'st *thou* aid mutinous Dutch, . . ."). On the other hand, considering its satirical intent, a useful approach to the poem may be to analyze it in terms of its similarities to an oration, a speech structured in part at least by considerations of its audience and delivered openly to that audience, who hears rather than overhears the speaker.

Let us turn first to Renaissance rhetorical theory, to the kind of theory Donne himself might have been familiar with, and then analyze "Satire III" in terms of that theory. Having looked at the poem rhetorically, we shall attempt to determine what its specifically poetical qualities are. We shall conclude by attempting to make specific suggestions concerning the rhetorical analysis of *modern* poems and stories.[4]

Of the three types of classical oratory (forensic, deliberative, and epideictic), this poem is most similar to deliberative oratory. Classically, deliberative oratory was political oratory, aimed at influencing the judgment of policy-determining assemblies. It was concerned with honorable action, the most honorable courses for men to take when faced with decisions. The classical rhetoricians knew that audiences are usually misled by prospects offering material advantage; therefore, they advised the orator that it would usually be necessary for him to distinguish for his audience between what is honorable and what is merely expedient. In the Renaissance, classical principles of deliberative oratory were applied to almost all the processes of public advice giving, exhortation, even sermonizing.[5]

Certainly this poem is full of exhortation and of attempts at persuasion. But one cannot go very far into the analysis of this poem as a deliberative oration until he answers two questions: Who comprise the audience addressed? And what important decisions are they faced with? Examining the arguments employed in lines 15-32 produces this picture of the audience: it is a youthful audience, to whom courage and valor must be expressed in terms of action, battle, and dueling; it is a lusty audience, eager for adventure and romance; in short, it shows the characteristics of young courtiers and gentlemen, the young men about London who are so prominent in Donne's other satires. These young gentlemen were most likely among the Londoners who could have read this poem soon after its completion, as it went the rounds, unsigned, in manuscript. Let us say, then, that young courtiers and gentlemen in sixteenth-century London are the audience. Obviously, the decisions they are faced with are religious decisions, but the precise nature of these decisions is only implied by the poem.

As we examine these decisions in an historical perspective and review Donne's arguments, we see that his actual thesis was potentially rebellious. The poem was written sometime between 1593 and 1597, in the fourth decade of the reign of Elizabeth I. Donne concludes his poem by exhorting his audience of young gentlemen not to follow the queen blindly and absolutely in religious matters—the sort of fealty the queen herself apparently desired, and the sort of allegiance most blindly or most fearfully given by the audience addressed.

By an act of supremacy Elizabeth had been given the same authority over the church as was assumed by her father. Like her father, she recognized the political advantage of this authority and sought to strengthen it by enforcing allegiance to the English Church throughout her realm, regarding all "recusants" as potential traitors, refusing university degrees to young students (Donne among them) who would not swear the oath of allegiance to the queen's supreme ecclesiastical authority, punishing Romanists (like Donne's younger brother, who in 1593 died of "gaol fever") and Puritans who refused to submit. Thus, the power of the throne is behind the phrase "forc'd but one allow" (l. 70).

At first, anxious to preserve her subjects' fanatical love for her while at the same time promoting internal harmony in the land (though any conjecture about Elizabeth's mind is at best problematical), the queen did not deal ruthlessly with Catholics, as later she was slow to act against the parliamentary tactics of the Puritans. But events of the 1580's—the discovery of the plots that surrounded Mary of Scotland, the Armada, growing agitation by Jesuits, the boldness of the Puritan Wentworth, Archbishop Whitgift's insistence on disciplinary measures—led her into an apparently firm resolve. As the nineties began, her course seemed to be firmly fixed on strengthening conformity to Anglicanism.

"Laws" were the weapons the queen and the Anglicans used against Catholics and Puritans as the nineties began. In 1593 "The Act Against Popish Recusants" considerably increased the efficiency of the surveillance and punishment of those Catholics who steadfastly refused to attend Protestant services. In the same year, Anglican defense of the English Church, particularly against Puritan arguments, began reaching a culmination with the publication of the first four books of Hooker's *Laws of Ecclesiastical Polity,* followed in 1597 by the publication of the fifth book. Catholics, of course, insisted on the supreme ecclesiastical authority of the Pope. Though Puritans, on the other hand, argued for a separation of church and state, their arguments actually envisioned a state led by their church. But Anglicans, through legal actions and theological arguments, with the sanctions of the queen, asserted the royal supremacy over church as well as state. It is in this scene—soon after 1593—a scene of religious and political turmoil controlled into tense order by the magnificent but tyrannical queen through "laws/ Still new like fashions," that the speaker of "Satire III" delivers his exhortations to young men close to the queen.

According to the rhetoricians, any speaker attempting such a task in such a situation must use the utmost discretion. In fact, "discretionary" was the word they used for the type of structure they advised for solving these problems of communication. The *traditional* way of arranging material in a deliberative oration was to divide the oration into these parts: entrance, narration, proposition, division, confirmation, confutation, and conclusion. The *discretionary* way consisted of only three parts: the orators were to place their best arguments first and last, "leaving the worst, in the middle of their speech altogether, the one to help the other; that with forcible things in the beginning, the auditors may be won; and with as good in the ending, have their mind and memory wholly occupied." So states the rhetorician Abraham Fraunce, who was a contemporary of Donne. In speaking on a cause that may not be acceptable to our hearers, states Fraunce, "it is not amiss, to imitate the cunning Surgeon, who hideth his knife, because his patient should not be discouraged." Let us divide the poem into four parts: an entrance and three major arguments. Without attempting a complete explication, let us examine the structure of these arguments. We shall find that it is in the last argument that the surgeon reveals his knife.

### ENTRANCE, LINES 1-4

The purpose of the entrance is to gain the audience's understanding and attention and to make them well disposed; for, according to the rhetorician Thomas Wilson, victory rests "first, in apt teaching the hearers, what the matter is, next in getting them to give good ear, and thirdly in winning their favor," and in accomplishing this the entrance is crucial. To gain the audience's understanding and attention in the entrance the orator may explain the nature of the case and its importance. One of the ways he may get their good will in the entrance is to reveal his own good character.

The speaker begins "Satire III" by indicating that his feelings toward the matter he is about to discuss are a compound of "kind pity" and "brave scorn": pity prevents him from laughing, scorn prevents him from weeping; therefore, in order to show sound judgment, he must neither laugh nor weep for these sins. To be true to his own feelings, he may not employ the lamenter's response to this subject nor even the rebuker's laugh. Since these are matters that call forth strong emotions, perhaps he can cure them by "railing." Yet, that course is of doubtful efficacy, since vigorous handling could not repair anything worn—and Donne soon shifts from railing to exhortation.

Thus, in one sentence, the speaker has opened his case by revealing at least three aspects of it. He has shown his own good character, as a man with a concern for the expression of sound judgment. He has shown that the case by its nature belongs to the general class of "sins" and "worn maladies" but that, considering his character and his own strong feelings, he finds the matter, though in part ridiculous, too serious for ridicule. It is this second aspect of the entrance that sets the tone for the entire poem. Moreover, this aspect rationalizes the speaker's "railing" by means of which he constructs the second part of his discourse. Finally, he shows the unfavorable light in which the case for the opposition will be displayed, as provoking both "spleen" and "tears," "scorn" and "pity."

## FIRST ARGUMENT, LINES 5–42

This argument narrows the speaker's case to the precise points at issue. As we might expect in an argument whose position indicates that it is one of the stronger arguments, the most direct appeals are made to the specific audience addressed.

That "our Mistress fair Religion" deserves "all our Soul's devotion" is proved in two parts: by comparing our (that is, the audience's) religious devotion with philosophical devotion in the "first blinded age," and by comparing our devotion to religion with our devotion to the pursuit of worldly gain and honor. In the first part, the speaker compares means, then ends. First comparing means: religion is as worthy of devotion as virtue in the ancient philosophy; "heaven's joys as valiant to assuage/ Lusts, as earth's honor." In drawing these four terms together, Donne means that the former should at least be able to perform the offices of the latter, because the former ("Religion," "heaven's joys") are greater. The force of his argument is strengthened by the epithet "first blinded age": that age (B.C.) was the *first* "blinded age," Donne's age is the second, for the second age is as blind to the Truth as it would be without the Light, Jesus, the Revelation of God's Truth. Then, comparing ends: shall the ancients' love of "earth's honor" be accounted more virtuous, more like the practice of Christian faith, than our "ways"—shall they be saved, while we are damned? Shall our fathers, who gave us the basic teachings of Christianity and thus made "easy" to perceive and "near" at hand (as compared to the Philosophers' ways) the instruments of our salvation, meet these Philosophers in heaven but learn of our damnation? Ironically, we may be damned for forsaking the basic, traditional doctrines and following instead other "easy and near ways," ways that require little effort or are politically expedient— the latter being underscored by the poem's conclusion.

In the second part, the speaker compares our devotion to religion with our devotion to the pursuit of worldly gain and honor, by proving this argument: fear of being damned involves greater courage and valor than do worldly pursuits, for indulging "Lusts" is actually a cowardly relinquishing to foes. Fear of being damned involves greater courage and valor than (1) adventurous enterprise, undertaken for gain, on the sea, aiding "mutinous Dutch" or becoming prey to the mysterious and unpredictable actions of man and nature, and on land, braving the extreme cold or the extreme heat, and (2) the exaggerated honor in amorous pursuits. The lover insisting that his mistress be called "Goddess" places his worldly mistress in ironic juxtaposition not only to "our Mistress fair Religion" but also to the ancients, whose mythological imagery was the rage of Renaissance lovers. Finally, the speaker reasons that fear of being damned involves greater courage and valor than do these pursuits, for these pursuits are the workings of our

foes—the devil, the world, and the flesh. Relinquishing ourselves to these foes is cowardice; it is a yielding to those
forces God gave us life and strength to battle.

## SECOND ARGUMENT, LINES 43-68

This argument deals with the question, Where should true
religion be sought? The speaker satirizes the answers men
have given to this question by dividing the answers into
Catholic and Protestant, Calvinist and Anglican, no
churches and all churches. Through this argument, the
speaker continues his "Mistress" metaphor for religion, a
metaphor that he introduced in the first argument. However, in the first argument, "Mistress" was used in an
idealized way, in the way one might speak of a lady as the
embodiment of virtue. In the second argument, "Mistress" becomes mere woman, real, earthy, unidealized.

It is important to note that Donne's barbs are aimed not
at churches but rather at the *reasons* men give for choosing
one church over the other. The "Mistress" metaphor in the
"Graius" example has added pungency when we remember
the audience and the situation of this poem. We should
note, too, the probable effect on the audience of the speaker's word "tender," the scornful opposite of "courage" and
"valor," virtues that are part of the real subject of the poem;
the scornfulness of "tender" might be particularly painful
to the youthful audience. The custom of paying "values,"
moreover, has in the England of this poem become law-
enforced fines for not attending the state-sanctioned
church.

## THIRD ARGUMENT, LINES 69-110

In this argument, religion is transformed from church into
faith, and the "Mistress" metaphor continues. Thus, the
"Mistress fair Religion," like the "profane" mistresses of

Donne's songs and sonnets, is both real and ideal: in this case, she is a real church and an ideal faith. The audience has forsaken the quest for the ideal, which, however, is attainable only through the real. In the first argument, he has insisted that religion is "worthy of all our Soul's devotion" and that therefore we must "Seek true religion"; his second argument has deplored the answers men have given to the question, Where should true religion be sought? In the final argument, he affirms two right ways by which true religion should be sought: (1) by actively seeking truth, deep assurances of our own convictions, or religious faith, and (2) by keeping the truth which we have found.

Whether we follow the lead of our own stable judgment or whether we are "forc'd," we must acknowledge one church, and the honorable thing to do, in either case, is to follow our conscience and acknowledge the "right" church. As for which is the right church, we should turn not only to our fathers but to our fathers' fathers, for "truth a little elder is" than the forced fashions and false passions of the age. In order to choose the right church, we must seek truth. In any "strange way," like the mysterious course of life, an active search for truth, not the blind acceptance of it or the course away from it, is the honorable path for man to follow. This is argued first in the allegory of Truth; and it is argued secondly in the exhortation to "therefore now do," for the "mind's endeavors" attain "hard knowledge" and the work of sorting out truth is the difficult job of seeking that whose contradiction another man may claim as truth. The speaker was being ironic as well as paradoxical and bitter when he claimed (ll. 68-69), echoing line 7, that "this blind-/ ness too much light breeds"—allowed to fashion our own reasons, we give up the search for truth and willingly turn our paths into "easy ways"; when he compares "mysteries" to the "Sun," he means again that all men may claim knowledge but all are actually dazzled by the source of knowledge.

Second, the speaker argues, "Keep the truth which thou hast found." Doing so is more honorable, more righteous, than following the dictates of temporal authority. This is argued in three ways: first, blindly following civil authority in spiritual matters could lead to damnation. Kings are not absolved of murder in killing those whom they hate; they are not deputies of God's will—"Vicars"—but merely executioners obeying the accidental laws of human destiny. It is wrong, then, for man to tie his soul to man's laws, by which the soul shall not be tried at the last day. Second, justifying one's choice by temporal authority, religious or civil—following the Catholic course simply because "a Philip, or a Gregory" or following the Protestant course simply because "A Harry, or a Martin" has taught one to— offers only reasons which all sides may use equally. Third, these arguments lead Donne into a definition of power, which when obeyed in matters that do not pertain to temporal authority produces "idolatry," the subversion of true religion. Power is likened to a stream, souls to flowers growing at the stream's edge; souls thrive, like flowers, when the "bounds" of power are kept, but perish in the "tyrannous rage" of the stream when the bounds are not kept. However, the flower is not the victim of its own choice; its vegetative principle is able only to select what it can feed on and avoid what it cannot (to "detest,/ And love," as the speaker says in Donne's "A Nocturnal Upon St. Lucy's Day," ll. 34-35). Flowers do not by their own force leave their roots or give themselves to the stream. But man's soul has this property. The difference—vivid to an audience brought up on the medieval doctrines of the vegetative, animal, and rational souls—enhances Donne's argument. Unlike flowers, man's soul has the property of moral choice, and by choosing man's power over God's the soul forfeits its immortality, a destruction as complete as that of a flower lost in the sea.

Thus, with strong "stirring of affections" the poem ends.

Let us examine Donne's thesis as revealed in the third, "knife-revealing" argument and in terms of the social context of this poem. As noted earlier, his thesis is potentially rebellious.

Donne's thesis is not pro-Catholic, nor pro-Puritan, nor pro-Anglican: "To adore, or scorn an image, or protest,/ May all be bad." His thesis is, rather, that in matters of religion we must follow the dictates of our conscience and that our conscience must be shaped by a firm conviction arrived at through reason ("the mind's endeavors"), tempered by tradition—and that the perversion of this truth seeking is idolatry, such as following the false gods of material gain or idolizing the decrees of temporal authority, civil or religious, in spiritual matters. In shaping his argument, the speaker finally strikes the greatest blow against all forces of temporal authority in spiritual matters and specifically against the most fearsome, most immediate of these forces. Kings are not "Vicars," but the speaker qualifies the boldness of his statement by placing kings with all who have assumed high authority over spiritual matters; the laws of man—Philip of Spain, Pope Gregory, Martin Luther, Henry VIII—take no precedence over the law of God, discoverable by the free, inquiring mind. But the most fearsome, most immediate obstacle to the activities of the mind embarked on such a search is subtly present and discernible to the audience: the power of Elizabeth. When Donne points directly, he uses masculine terms: "Harry" (l. 97), "Kings" (l. 91), "Prince" (l. 48). But all the feminine references, which dominate the poem, are not to be explained away as poetic convention or as signs of Donne's own amorousness. He names Elizabeth for what she is: "Power," whose bounds we must know for the health of our souls—she is thus directly opposed to "our Mistress fair Religion"—and calling Power "her" throughout lines 100-102 would surely be, for the satire's audience, a sharply clear, even literal personification. Souls perish when men so courageous and valorous in less vital quests, humbly give themselves to the "tyrannous rage" of the queen in matters that are not part of her natural prerogative—when natural order is usurped, when power is not "rightly" obeyed. To the idea noted earlier in the final image—that flowers, unlike men's souls, cannot be victims of their own moral choice—may be added the picture of a stream allowed to overflow its banks.

It is illuminating to read the last lines of this poem, in which Donne compares Elizabeth-Power to a stream, in light of the following lines from "Satire V" (ll. 28-30):

> Greatest and fairest Empress, know you this?
> Alas, no more than Thames' calm head doth know
> Whose meads her arms drown, or whose corn o'rflow:

Donne, wondering whether Elizabeth knows of the corruption in her court, compares her again to the "calm head" of a stream. Though when two poems are brought together one must serve only to illuminate rather than to explain the other, it is perhaps also significant that a few years after he wrote "Satire III," Donne was at work on his most ambitious satire, "Progress of the Soul," in which he planned to trace the passage of the soul of heresy from Eve's apple to Queen Elizabeth. The illumination which this affords is to serve as a reminder that it was not until after the first decade of the seventeenth century, so crucial in the turbulent religious history of Donne the man, that Donne the poet could reveal an appreciation of Elizabeth as head of both state and church. In "Satire III" and "Satire V," his *personae* speak of Elizabeth as the "calm head" of a stream; as applied in the satires, the image works two ways: in "Satire III," she is part of the natural order but only as head of *state* and, as such, her bounds must be known and kept; in "Satire V," she is, even as head of state, insensitive to and unaffected by the corruption in her own court.

Thus, with the power of Elizabeth as an adversary and

before an audience of his young contemporaries, the speaker of "Satire III" displays his true "wit" and "discretion" in rhetorical proving. So far as the identity of the speaker is concerned—in rhetorical terminology, his *ethos*—Donne's strategy is not to call attention to the speaker's specific personality traits but to give evidence of his character through the moral values in his argument. Donne's ethical appeals depend not on some dramatized personality but on the moral values built into an argument carefully constructed to cause those young men at the rough stream's calm head to look within their own characters.

To evaluate "Satire III" as rhetoric would require some assessment of the effect it might have had on the audience addressed and some assessment of the ethical or moral value of the arguments within the context of Donne's society. However, neither of these assessments would give us much indication of those qualities which have caused people to take pleasure or interest in this poem even though they are not the audience addressed and even though they may have only partially understood the poem. Some of these qualities are more akin to poetic than to rhetoric, and, oddly enough, a rhetorical analysis may help us view more clearly the peculiarly poetical qualities of the utterance. One of these qualities is obvious even upon casual reading: richness of imagination. The ideas in this poem are rich, many-layered, multivalent in concept, transcending the specific subject of the search for true religion. The images are vivid and associative. However, *artistic structure* is the most general poetical quality of this poem, as of all poems; and how the ideas and images are put together, organized, in this poem has seldom been fully realized in critical analyses that have been narrowly nonrhetorical. Many critics have argued that this poem is rough in structure, interesting not artistically but only for the reason that it was composed by a great poet. Some critics have argued that, though structurally rough, the poem is richly imaginative. One critic, referred to earlier, in an attempt to view the poem's structural artistry saw this poem as a soliloquy, the ideas and images being associated by a mind as it attempts to arrive at a resolution of a problem—perhaps a typically "poetic" view for our age. Our rhetorical analysis gives us another view of the artistry of the structure: the poem was carefully and skillfully put together in order to produce an effect on a specific audience. This rhetorical view gives us insight into the poetry of the utterance, for it lets us see not only the basic principle of structure but also the full richness of Donne's imagination as it operated within the limitations imposed by audience and situation— and these two, the principle and the limitations, best define any feeling of "wholeness."

The particular kind of structural artistry which this poem has was best named by a nineteenth-century critic and poet who loved to read Donne aloud. Samuel Taylor Coleridge called the beauty a "manly harmony." [6] In his notes on seventeenth-century poets, Coleridge advised, "Read even Donne's Satires as he meant them to be read, and as the sense & passion demand, and you will find in the lines a manly harmony." Coleridge said "even" Donne's satires, for of all the older poems, including plays, the meter of Donne's satires must have sounded particularly rough to a post-Dryden age of metrical smoothness. Unfortunately, Coleridge did not leave behind any interpretation of what he understood the "sense & passion" of Donne's satires to be. So far as "Satire III" is concerned, our rhetorical analysis would indicate that the "sense & passion" demand an *oratorical* delivery, that the poem should sound like public argument being forcefully delivered to an audience.

Concerning "Satire III" Coleridge did say, "If you would teach a scholar in the highest form how to *read,* take Donne, and of Donne this satire. When he has learnt to read

Donne, with all the force and meaning which are involved in the words, then send him to Milton, and he will stalk on like a master *enjoying* his walk." Learning to read this poem aloud—or, to put it as simply and as emphatically as Coleridge did, learning to *read* this poem—is still instructive, for the very reason Coleridge may have had in mind: the discipline required in getting and keeping the thought, in controlling vocal force to achieve the requisite emphasis, and in achieving and refining one's awareness of Donne's structure—these lead one to a knowledge of Donne's sense of symmetry, his "manly harmony," whereby he joined vigorous argument with ordered beauty through rhythm, sound, arrangement. Learning to *read* this poem may be *corrective,* too, for it may allow us, brought up as we were in an age when critics would have us think of poetry in terms of the soliloquy and not in terms of the oration, to recover a sense of and perhaps even appreciation for the voice of poets who speak openly to men of their own age. To hear Milton's voice, for example, something more is needed than Romantic doctrines which make individual man a unique and lonely entity and which make poetry "the spontaneous overflow of powerful feelings." And not only Milton's voice, but Wordsworth's, too.

# III

In making a rhetorical analysis of Renaissance literature, we have several advantages that we apparently do not have when we attempt to make a rhetorical analysis of modern literature. We have, for example, several rhetorical theories that we might employ in the analysis of any one literary work. We have the textbooks of Wilson, Fraunce, Fenner, MacIlmaine—the Ciceronians, the Scholastics, the Ramists. We have the advantage of a perspective created by our removal in time. We have the knowledge that we are dealing with a more or less "coherent" period, characterized by concepts of order and degree, and, in certain matters, absolute value, making it easier for us to study convention and custom. We have the knowledge that there was an admitted connection between rhetoric and poetry; the poets learned from the rhetoricians and rhetoricians learned from the poets—many of the rhetoricians illustrated their theories with passages of poetry. How, then, could we possibly apply the principles illustrated in this chapter to the analysis of modern literature?

A modern literary historian in writing on the sixteenth century states that it is the appreciation of rhetoric which marks the greatest barrier between ourselves and our ancestors.[7] He seems to think of rhetoric, however, as pertaining to style—figures and conceits. If we were to return to a more accurate concept of rhetoric in the Renaissance, when it was not always equated merely with stylistic devices, we may discover that the barrier has never really existed—and can never exist so long as poetry itself is prized —though the conscious appreciation of rhetoric has long disappeared from our critical analyses. Such a discovery may have been at the basis of the remarks on Donne made by Coleridge's contemporary critic and poet, Thomas De Quincey. De Quincey called Donne "the first very eminent rhetorician in the English literature" and informed his readers that in calling Donne a rhetorician he was referring not to Donne's style but to his "management of the thoughts."[8]

Rhetoric has fallen into unnecessary disrepute and disuse in our critical doctrines, mostly because of a misunderstanding of what rhetoric actually is. In some critical doctrines, "rhetoric" is used to mean purple patches, or dishonesty, or deception, or aesthetically neutral elements, like grammar and syntax. Only recently have some critics endeavored to use rhetoric in its older meaning, as a persuasive faculty and as an art of communication, a discipline concerned generally with the management of thoughts—

ideas and values—in a discourse. Prominent among these critics is Wayne C. Booth, who in his analysis of fiction arrives at the sensible conclusion that the literary artist cannot reject rhetoric, he can only decide what kind of rhetoric to use.[9] This is not to make every artist into a hack writer, catering to popular taste, or into a crusader, burning brilliantly while a few short-fused social issues are still smoldering. It is to state that every literary work which men read and understand may have within it some communicative principle which can be analyzed—and should be assimilated consciously into our appreciation of the work. Whether the principle is there by design does not matter. Every literary work presents a speaker within a certain situation, who is either being heard or being overheard by an audience, and how he engages that audience and, ultimately, us is as proper a concern of the literary critic as any other literary aspect. And much of that concern is properly considered rhetorical.

There is a sense in which *all* literature that is read, understood, and enjoyed is rhetorical, if we allow "rhetorical" for the moment to mean generally the process whereby a speaker *of* or *in* any literary work engages a reader. Many of our modern lyrics are soliloquies, in which a speaker utters his thoughts aloud to himself with no consideration of an audience. It is apparently most modern to think of the soliloquy as the most truly "poetical" speaking situation and, by extension, of the lyric as the essence of poetry. Yet no work of literature, not even a soliloquy, can succeed until it *does* find *an* audience, and that process whereby it engages us and makes us its audience may be either analogous to or identical with rhetoric. Take our responses to a soliloquy, T. S. Eliot's "The Love Song of J. Alfred Prufrock," and to a monologue, Andrew Marvell's "To His Coy Mistress." An audience is not ostensibly present in Eliot's poem, and *only* ostensibly present in Marvell's. Yet it has been the experience of modern readers that in overhearing Prufrock's soliloquy, we have responded by identifying even more strongly with the speaker than we might if we were actually addressed by him. In Marvell's "To His Coy Mistress," the audience is only ostensibly present, for the speaker also soliloquizes and, like Prufrock, touches responsive chords in his readers, those men of Marvell's time or of our own time who only overhear the speaker but who either, with him, share a melancholy view of existence or can be deeply affected by the skillful structuring of thoughts on complex problems of existence.

The poet, as Lawrence Ferlinghetti wrote, is like an acrobat, who in performing "above the heads/ of his audience" risks "absurdity/ and death." [10] Ferlinghetti's voice gives the idea a modern sound. Yet there is nothing modern, unfortunately, in a plea to admire the very means whereby the poet in taking that risk manages to survive. In 1647 James Shirley addressed the reader of Beaumont and Fletcher's *Comedies and Tragedies* with this observation: "You may find passions raised to that excellent pitch and by such insinuating degrees that you shall not choose but consent, and go along with them, finding yourself at last grown insensibly the very same person you read, and then stand admiring the subtle tracks of your engagement." [11] The literary artist could not find better praise. The admiration of these tracks should be no less a part of our literary appreciation than it was for our ancestors.

But, given the condition that no poem ever achieves meaning or survives until it finds an audience, we have so far discussed matters that are not *necessarily* rhetorical, matters that may be only confusing to call rhetorical. A poem may engage a reader by being artistically structured, or its engaging a reader may depend upon the reader's having the requisite sensitivity and taste to enjoy the poem. Perhaps some of these matters are best thought of as belonging to the craft of poetry, or are matters to be solved by the literary education of poets and readers. Though these matters are analogous to rhetoric (and might be called "rhetoricalistic" but for the awkwardness of the term), it is least confusing to confine rhetoric to our examination of those works which are structured in terms of a speaker-audience situation.

Speakers, audiences, and issues dealt with in a literary work may be specific or general, real or imaginary, implied or named. These qualities determine whether the rhetoric in the work is imaginary or actual. The more general and imaginary the audience and the more universal are the issues dealt with in the work, the more imaginary the rhetoric in it. The more specific and real the audience and the more specific and real the issues dealt with in the work, the more actual the rhetoric in it. *The rhetorical analysis is concerned with the interaction of speaker, audience, and issues, as that interaction becomes a structuring principle of the literary work.* "Satire III" is a good example of a work that is *actually* rhetorical and at the same time poetical, a work whose poetical qualities arise from an artistic use of the rhetorical faculty.

Three steps should be taken to employ the rhetorical analysis in an examination of those works which are structured in terms of a speaker-audience situation.

First, we try to find the characteristics of the person who is speaking and of the audience to whom he is speaking. This situation may be largely imaginary or real. The speaker's characteristics may be only suggested, as in "Satire III." Or the range of types may extend to a fully dramatized character—as, say, the duke who speaks Robert Browning's "My Last Duchess." The speaker may be someone we are meant to trust, like the speaker of "Satire III," or distrust, like Browning's duke. The audience, too, may be only implied, as in "Satire III," or named, as in the Browning poem.

Second, it is on the basis of analyzing this speaker-audience situation that we attempt to understand the strategies of communication in the poem. Whether the speaker is one we or the audience, named or implied, are meant to trust or distrust, we look for signs in the poem which establish character—the fierce pride of the duke, the desire for freedom of conscience expressed by the speaker of "Satire III." Whether the audience is named or implied, we compare its characteristics with our own, as we usually do when we make the imaginative effort to participate in a poem and imagine the effects on the audience of the speaker's utterance. For example, in Jesse Stuart's "Love," the narrator addresses an implied audience informally and familiarly, assuming that they will know certain things and share certain attitudes:

> Yesterday when the bright sun blazed down on the wilted corn my father and I walked around the edge of the new ground to plan a fence. The cows kept coming through the chestnut oaks on the cliff and running over the young corn. They bit off the tips of the corn and trampled down the stubble.[12]

In Lord Dunsany's "The Ghosts," the narrator speaks to an implied audience of some sophistication:

> Then there entered two by two the high-born ladies and their gallants of Jacobean times. They were little more than shadows—very dignified shadows, and almost indistinct; but you have all read ghost stories before, you have all seen in museums the dresses of those times—there is little need to describe them; they entered, several of them, and sat down on the old chairs. . . .[13]

In both of these examples, what the narrator says is determined in part by the characteristics of the implied audience—structure is a strategy for engaging that audience. As readers, we sometimes see, sometimes become, the audience in the work. If the audience is specific and real, as in "Satire III," we need to see it in order to understand the work. If the audience is general and imaginary, not only do we need to see the audience, but oftentimes we make ourselves over into that audience—as if the author had given us a role we must perform in the communication of the poem. Part of our pleasure as readers may lie in finding that role and playing it, entering willingly and sometimes irresistibly into the communicative situation the author has created.

Third, again, as in our analysis of "Satire III," we may examine a work's structure from a point *extrinsic* to it, from some actual rhetorical theory, regarding the work primarily as an act of communication between the writer and his readers. In this case it is the *author* and *his* audience that we are directly concerned with, though for all purposes in practical criticism these may be the speaker and audience *in* the work. A body of theory, called "rhetoric," exists today. I. A. Richards is one of its exponents; so is Kenneth Burke. Burke has done much work in applying in literary analysis a fusion of rhetorical and poetical concepts, a fusion similar to the "contextual" analysis employed in the following chapter. Furthermore, many of our modern writers have developed and expressed their own theories of communication. In his notebooks, Henry James evolves a rhetorical theory based on the intensity whereby men of his time may experience an illusion that real life has been presented in his fiction. T. S. Eliot's work has been examined in light of his doctrine of "objective correlative" —a doctrine that allows us to see the operation of rhetoric even in Eliot's soliloquies if we can identify that audience Eliot's doctrine seems most vividly aware of. Other writers—such as Flannery O'Connor, with her statements on the function of "grotesqueness" in her fiction—have commented on their craft in such a way that at times they indicate what they take to be their strategies for engaging a certain reader's mind and senses. And it is also true that many writers have as *artists* expressed utter contempt for rhetoric or have ignored all discussions of the communicative dimensions of their work—but as readers we can do neither.

As oral readers, faced in part with the task of communicating literature to others, we may derive considerable help from the rhetorical analysis. We may find those strategies we will need when as practising rhetoricians in our introductions we seek to make our own audience see or become the audience in or of the work. For centuries rhetoricians have taught that appropriateness of delivery is always dictated by the components of the speaking situation—the speaker, the audience, and the speech, particularly. A rhetorical analysis, in which we examine the speaker and audience *in* a work or in which we examine the rhetorical strategies by which the *author* engages his readers, should help us find an appropriate style of delivery, one that may in turn be appropriate for *our own* speaking situation. Hopefully, the rhetorical analysis will help us avoid the fallacy of assuming that artistic utterance can be accomplished only within a soliloquizing privacy.

## NOTES

1. R. S. Crane, *The Languages of Criticism and the Structure of Poetry* (Toronto: University of Toronto Press, 1953), p. 43. See also Elder Olson, "An Outline of Poetic Theory," in Ronald S. Crane, ed., *Critics and Criticism,* abridged ed. (Chicago: Phoenix, 1957), Ch. I.

2. N. J. C. Andreasen, "Theme and Structure in Donne's *Satyres," Studies in English Literature,* III (Winter 1963), 59-75.

3. The text of the poem follows the edition by Herbert J. C. Grierson, *The Poems of John Donne,* I (London: Oxford University Press, 1912), 154-158. I have mod-

ernized the spelling but, with the exception of the apostrophe, left the punctuation and capitalization as in Grierson's edition. Renaissance punctuation and capitalization, as in this poem, are frequently excellent guides to the voice.

4. The following analysis appeared, in different form, in *Quarterly Journal of Speech,* LI (Feb. 1965), 14-27. I am indebted to the editor of that journal for allowing me to reuse some of the material.

5. The rhetoricians quoted in this discussion are Abraham Fraunce, *The Lawiers Logike* (London, 1588), and Thomas Wilson, *The Arte of Rhetorique* (London, 1553). For a study of the history of Renaissance rhetoric, see Wilbur Samuel Howell, *Logic and Rhetoric in England, 1500-1700* (Princeton, N. J.: Princeton University Press, 1956).

6. Roberta Florence Brinkley, ed., *Coleridge on the Seventeenth Century* (Durham, N. C.: Duke University Press, 1955), pp. 521, 654.

7. C. S. Lewis, *English Literature in the Sixteenth Century Excluding Drama* (London: Oxford University Press, 1954), p. 61.

8. Thomas De Quincey, "Rhetoric," *The Works of Thomas De Quincey* (Boston: Houghton Mifflin and Co., 1876), IV, 330-332.

9. Wayne C. Booth, *The Rhetoric of Fiction* (Chicago: University of Chicago Press, 1961).

10. Lawrence Ferlinghetti, "15," *A Coney Island of the Mind* (New York: New Directions, 1958), p. 30.

11. James Shirley, "To the Reader," *Comedies and Tragedies Written by Francis Beaumont and John Fletcher, Gentlemen* (London, 1647), sig. A₃ᵛ.

12. Jesse Stuart, "Love," in Cleanth Brooks and Robert Penn Warren, *Understanding Fiction,* 2d ed. (New York: Appleton-Century-Crofts, 1959), p. 293.

13. Lord Dunsany, "The Ghosts," in Milton Crane, ed., *Fifty Great Short Stories* (New York: Bantam, 1952), p. 402.

RECOMMENDED READING

A good starting point, a good general discussion of the subject, is still Hoyt H. Hudson's "Rhetoric and Poetry." Having appeared as a journal article forty years ago, it is probably most readily available in *Historical Studies of Rhetoric and Rhetoricians,* ed. Raymond F. Howes (Ithaca: Cornell University Press, 1961), pp. 369-379.

Cleanth Brooks and Robert Penn Warren, in *Understanding Fiction* (listed above), frequently make rhetorical approaches to fiction; see especially their analyses of Lardner's "Haircut," pp. 136-150, and Hemingway's "The Killers," pp. 296-312.

For examples of rhetorical approaches to poems, see Irene H. Chayes, "Rhetoric as Drama: An Approach to the Romantic Ode," *PMLA,* LXXIX (March 1964), 67-79, and John M. Wallace, "Marvell's Horatian Ode," *PMLA,* LXXVII (March 1962), 33-45.

Insofar as the rhetorical analysis places the author in a narrowly conceived role as communicator, creating his structures mostly through the "looking-outward" (as opposed to introspection) that communication implies, then the shortcomings of the rhetorical analysis must be acknowledged and guarded against. But to say this is partly to utter the old truism that art is too complex to be embraced by any one analysis. An interesting place to begin correcting the potential errors of the rhetorical view is in the philosophical and critical works that assign the writer a didactic but distinctly nonrhetorical role: e.g., William Barrett, "The Testimony of Modern Art," *Irrational Man* (New York: Anchor, 1962), Ch. 3, and Norman O. Brown, "Art and Eros," *Life Against Death: The Psychoanalytical Meaning of History* (New York: Vintage, n.d.), Ch. 5.

R. S. Crane's *The Languages of Criticism and the Structure of Poetry* (listed above) is an attempt to formulate by Aristotelian method a distinctly "poetical" approach to the analysis of literature; see especially the essay entitled "Poetic

Structure in the Language of Aristotle," and for the application of these attitudes in practical criticism, see the second chapter of the present book. For an interesting "conjecture" concerning a method Aristotle might have used for the rhetorical analysis of literature, see footnote 57 in the Crane book, p. 197.

## Projects

The following projects may be used as the bases for short papers analyzing selections to be read aloud in class. Except where noted, all of the poems and stories in the following projects may be found in Oscar Williams, ed., *Immortal Poems of the English Language* (New York: Washington Square, 1952) and Milton Crane, ed., *Fifty Great Short Stories* (New York: Bantam, 1952).

1. What are the characteristics of the implied audience(s) in the following short poems? "Farewell to Love" by Michael Drayton, "The Flea" by John Donne, "Death the Leveller" by James Shirley, "Dover Beach" by Matthew Arnold, "Poetry" by Marianne Moore, and "Ultima Ratio Regum" by Stephen Spender. How may you get your own audience either to see or to become the implied audience(s)?

2. We have described the soliloquy as the process whereby man in solitude structures his own private thoughts. Oftentimes, however, this process can have certain public qualities—as if the speaker were aware that his contemplation were being overheard by others, a "potential" rather than implied audience.

   a. Analyze the poem "The Road Not Taken" by Robert Frost as basically a soliloquy but one that the speaker knows is being overheard by people brought up on the parable of the "straight and narrow road" that leads to eternal happiness. However, don't be misled into believing that the speaker's true subject is religion. Imagine the effects on the "potential" audience. What are the clues to tone?

b. Of all poets in the modern mold, Emily Dickinson is one we should most likely consider not only non-rhetorical but even disengaged from the society around her. Yet a critic has shown that much illumination can be afforded by interpreting her poems as responses to intellectual and moral conventions of her own society: Charles R. Anderson, *Emily Dickinson's Poetry: Stairway of Surprise* (New York: Holt, Rinehart, and Winston, 1960). Read Anderson's interpretation of her "I Heard a Fly Buzz When I Died": he calls it "an ironic reversal of the conventional attitudes of her time and place toward the significance of the moment of death" (p. 232). Analyze the poem by imagining the effects the poem might have had on those people who held these "conventional attitudes." If we view this as a poem structured by the speaker's awareness of the unconventionality of her attitudes when perceived from certain standpoints in her potential audience, what parts of the poem become particularly emphatic?

3. Read the short story "The Garden Party" by Katherine Mansfield. What values does the narrator assume he shares with his audience? Can you build a case for proving that the narrator is in secret communion with his audience behind the backs of his characters? In this respect, note particularly the paragraph that begins "That really was extravagant . . ." Would you say that the narrator has only contempt for Laura? What is the function of Laurie in the story? Examine carefully the last two paragraphs. What is the narrator's attitude when he says, "He quite understood"?

4. Read the short story "For Esmé—With Love and Squalor" by J. D. Salinger. This is the story that the narrator promised Esmé he would write for her someday. But notice that in the structure of the story he does not address Esmé until the very end, and notice too that he states that his intentions are "to edify, to instruct." His thesis is, as one critic put it quite simply, that love is the emotional therapy for the squalor of wartime experiences. But in teaching us that thesis, part of the narrator's strategy is to make us sympathetic with his own character. How easy is it for us to become the kind of audience the narrator wants us to be, one that will sympathize with his character? Note every appeal for sympathy that the narrator makes—his humor, his gas-mask container full of books, his singling out Esmé in the choir, etc. Why does the narrator switch from first person to third person? Why does he introduce his disguise with irony? Note that throughout the story we are asked to join in secret communion with the narrator against various forces in society.

5. An analysis of Flannery O'Connor's short story "Everything That Rises Must Converge" (title story of her last collection, published by Farrar, Straus & Giroux, New York, in 1965) could be fully rhetorical. Find statements which Miss O'Connor has made concerning her own rhetorical theories, particularly those concerning the efficaciousness of "grotesqueness" and concerning the audience for whom she wrote. Analyze carefully the sympathies of the narrator in this story. Would you say that he is completely sympathetic with the boy? his mother? the Negro? all or none? Where does he seem to stand on the social issue which has precipitated the conflict? Are the narrator's strategies illuminated by the social context of the story? How have these strategies determined the structure of the story?

## CHAPTER FIVE

# BIOGRAPHICAL-SOCIAL
# ANALYSIS:
## The Symbolic Act in Its Context,
## Chekhov's "Ward No. 6"

*MARK S. KLYN*

## I

The essential core of literary study, for the oral interpreter as for all readers, is the intrinsic approach to the work itself, the close reading and explication of the text. The reader must first seek to go deeply into works of literature by analyzing them through methods limited by their particular verbal forms, bounding his perspectives, for the sake of focus, to the text. The New Criticism's most valuable service, surely, has been its demonstration of this: the poem itself must be first and foremost the object of criticism and contemplation, for it alone is the source of all its meaning and its value.

Yet with this much admitted—and indeed held as a principle constantly to be honored—it is still possible to argue with the insularity which is a consequence of too absolute a commitment to this principle. Some of its advocates would see the text not only as the core of literary study, but as the only, and self-limiting, factor in such study. Such monistic critics would really aggrandize the text-centered framework from a focus on *what* should be studied into a prescription on *how* it should be studied, and it is this limitation which is debatable.

Other critics, then, have sought ways to go beyond the intrinsic into the use of extrinsic modes of analysis, which try to illuminate literary works by considering them in the light of frames of reference external to themselves. Kenneth Burke, implementing his maxim, "The main ideal of criticism, as I conceive it, is to use all that is there to use," is perhaps the most effective theorist of a more eclectic criticism. And R. P. Blackmur, though he is quite different from Burke, is perhaps its most effective practitioner.

Such reformers of the text-centered critical framework, while of course agreeing that the work of literature is the essential point, would contend really that criticism should entertain a larger conception of what the "work" is. Thinking of literature, in George Steiner's sense, "as existing not in isolation but as central to the play of historical and political energies," [1] they conceive an "open-ended" criticism. A literary work, they would hypothesize, may involve far more than its words and images stabilized in structure; its formed unity may hold in momentary balance many forces and tensions connecting it with worlds outside itself, and its deepest life and meaning may even lie in these connections. Thus, they would argue that a work of literature may be validly approached from any sort of extrinsic standpoint which can illuminate it, that the critical process though it must begin in intrinsic analysis as a *sine qua non* need not end in it, and that the measure of criticism should be the insight that results, not its conformity to any *a priori* definitions.

It is on such a set of hypotheses that this essay rests. The intrinsic approach would abstract the text from its context, gaining its focus and concentration by exploiting the construct that the literary work is a self-contained entity, timeless and complete within itself. And while this sort of focus is helpful for analysis at the start, its premises are also palpably unreal, and the construct they form is too restrictive to be convenient beyond the beginning stages of criticism.

If, on the other hand, one follows Burke in thinking that criticism should consider the literary work as the "symbolic act" of the artist, one is led inevitably toward an opening to the extrinsic. An "act" is necessarily interested and functional, and happens within a concrete, relevant context. (If it is merely reflexive or incoherent, an action may be arresting, but it could not be "art.") Thus, the "meaning" of an act must, more or less, be found in the field of its relationships with its context. And some works will go even further and aim purposively to affect the reality in which they exist—being, in this sense, "actual rhetoric," as discussed in the preceding chapter. In any case, a Burkean synthesis would leap the traditional Aristotelian distinction between rhetoric and poetic, to find a rhetorical component in almost any sort of "act."

(Admittedly, there is something necessarily anarchic about such a non-Aristotelian formulation. Once the critic opens his analysis outward in this way, to seek the full contextual meaning of the work, where is he to stop? Theoretically, nowhere. The only limiting factors would be the validity of the insights reached into the work and the critic's ability to synthesize these insights. But in respect to literature, this degree of multifariousness does not seem to me a bad thing—even if it entails some cost in clarity.)

Thinking of works of literature as conscious attempts of writers to grapple with their realities, the critic would try essentially to define the writer's particular interrelationship with his world, thus to discover the terms in which the writer's "act" has meaning. And it is best to be as concrete and realistic in this as possible, thinking first of the work in its own time and place and resisting the temptation to generalize on more abstract levels before a basis has been set. Many literary works are resonant with grander, more universal meanings beyond their particularity. But in working toward these meanings, one must take care not merely to "philosophize," or to operate in grandiose extrapolations, or to make the writer over into an ideologue, or worst of all to make him a spokesman for one's own beliefs so that criticism becomes only persuasion disguised. For the critic, the literary work should never be merely grist for the mill of his own preconceptions, and concreteness, temporality, and particularity are safeguards against critical self-serving.

Critical disinterestedness, though, should not become indifference masked as objectivity. Writers are first men, like the rest of us, and their lives too are anxious and inconclusive "arguments with existence," in Lawrence Ferlinghetti's phrase. They too quarrel with themselves and their finiteness—the limits of their consciousnesses and the inevitability of death—and with the world in which they must live. But, unlike the rest of us, they are moved to make art out of these encounters. And literature, in this view, arises out of the artist's need to know and to evaluate, to find the order and meaning of his existence: as James Baldwin has put it, "I write to make sense out of my life."

Writers, to put it another way, exist in social and historical contexts which define the limits against which they must strive, and literary works are born of the tension inherent in this matrix. "Only connect," E. M. Forster once said. The function of the extrinsic critic is essentially to find the "connections" linking the work with its context. (If they exist, it goes without saying. Sometimes the critic may not wish to seek for such connections, for in terms of a particular writer's work they may not be important. Some artists—austere, dedicated, or timid beings, living for their

art and isolating themselves in it—try to avoid this tension, or to transcend it, in their works. And criticism
would be inept if it tried to take such writing on any but its
own terms.)

Many influences, obviously, act on the writer to shape his
work and will be reflected in it, and there are many possible connections. Clearly, no discrete critical method will
serve, and a good deal will depend on the sensibility and
judgment of the critic. This breadth of possibilities is actually the main problem, and it must be allowed that, if
one cares a great deal for methodological rigor and severity, the attitude toward criticism advanced here is too uncertain and had best be avoided. The only trouble, I think,
is that a great deal may be missed. Still, even within the
plenitude of potential extrinsic standpoints, perhaps it is
possible to suggest some priorities.

The most important factors operating to shape the writer's work will probably be the determining moments of his
life, the most immediate field in which his unique consciousness is forged, and the social *milieu* in which he tempers
his consciousness. More specifically, the forming influences
of the *milieu* will consist in the field of intellectual, political, and religious forces which are important in his world
and to which his work is a response.

The tensions between the writer's life in society and his
art, his connection with his particular contextual field, can
be seen in a vital way in the work of Chekhov. And I want
to try to consider his novella "Ward No. 6" to suggest some
of the relevance and point of the critical direction I've tried
to indicate here. Indeed, I should think that any sort of full
apprehension of the meaning of "Ward No. 6" is unlikely
without some working of this standpoint, for the story
seems to me a wholly engaged piece of work, vitally involved with its world and drawing its force from the passion of this involvement.

# II

Many critics, perhaps influenced by the political bifurca-
tion of our world, would seek to rescue Chekhov for the
West by isolating him from his own time and place and
would resist the point of view I shall suggest. The most
common view of Chekhov would see him as the melancholy—though often partly comic—bemused poet of a dying world, affectionately imaging its weary, fragile affinities
and evasions with tender charm: "The Voice of Twilight
Russia," in Princess Toumanova's phrase.[2] Thus, with a sort
of ex post facto fixity, some critics would interpret everything which immediately preceded the Russian Revolution
as shadowed in catastrophe. Finding in Chekhov's humor
an index of resignation, and blind to the rebelliousness of
his irony, many critics tend, as Irving Howe writes, "to
roll onto their backs and purr."[3]

To be sure, a sort of humorous acceptance can be seen as
one of the tones in some of Chekhov's plays and stories—
though one would have to be obtuse not to see the irony
with which Chekhov usually undercuts it. But resignation,
tender or apathetic, is not a dominant strain in Chekhov's
work, and it would be as much in error to interpret "Ward
No. 6" in the mood of *The Cherry Orchard* as to see *Macbeth* in terms of *The Tempest*. On the contrary, for most of
his life Chekhov was a man forcefully engaged with his
world, vitally alive in his time, and a writer who made criticism of his society the spine of his art. Even in dying, acceptance was foreign to him: his last story, "Betrothed,"
written when Chekhov was caught in the last stages of tuberculosis, is one of his most iconoclastic, forward-looking
works. But the quality of his engagement was special, and
its uniqueness lies at the heart of his writing.

No writer was more undoctrinaire and unpolemical
than Chekhov. His repeated testimony shows that he made

objectivity and veracity a central aesthetic principle and despised special pleading in art.[4] He was no disciple of any program or system and distrusted those who were—even Tolstoy, whom he loved. It is true that Chekhov's relationship with Tolstoy and his ideology was ambivalent: for a time during the 1880's Chekhov was an ardent "Tolstoyan," but he soon became disillusioned and in later years, though he retained his love and respect for Tolstoy himself, Chekhov found his ideas most inadequate. But he never ceased to matter a great deal to Chekhov. Tolstoy's moral authority was so great that his influence was inevitable, and even his most obviously unsound ideas had to be taken seriously. Thus, Chekhov habitually measured his own thinking against Tolstoy's and was continually reacting against him—much as Strindberg found it impossible not to temper himself against Ibsen. This almost *had* to be true: it was Tolstoy's genius to dominate his age, and he was a major contextual influence on nearly every thoughtful person in nineteenth-century Russia.

But aside from his flirtation with Tolstoy's philosophy, no writer of the age was more adamantly resistant than Chekhov to what Isaiah Berlin has called "the tyranny of the great altruistic systems"[5]—the all-consuming, all-encompassing utopian philosophies of reform and redemption which continually swept pre-Revolutionary Russia, exhausting the creative energies of their partisans in megalomaniacal dreams and internecine squabbling. The tenacity of his commitment to independence and freedom was formidable:

> I am afraid of those who look for a tendency between the lines, and who are determined to regard me either as a liberal or as a conservative. I am not a liberal, not a conservative, not a believer in gradual progress, not a monk, not an indifferentist. I should like to be a free artist and nothing more, and I regret that God has

not given me the power to be one. I hate lying and violence in all their forms, . . . I have no preference either for gendarmes, or for butchers, or for scientists, or for writers, or for the younger generation. I regard trademarks and labels as a superstition. My holy of holies is the human body, health, intelligence, talent, inspiration, love, and the most absolute freedom—freedom from violence and lying, whatever forms they may take. This is the programme I would follow if I were a great artist. (*Letters*, p. 127) *

Yet, surely, Chekhov's very independence and his hatred of abstractions and systems which forgot the primacy of the human personality were, in themselves, an ethic and in his world a truly radical "philosophy." As the above-quoted passage also indicates, Chekhov began at "the end of ideology," in Daniel Bell's phrase, but moved not toward disengagement but into an elemental, nondoctrinal humanism. Especially after 1890, Chekhov was a wholly responsive and humane writer. And no artist was less attracted by notions of aesthetic detachment from the life around him, or more contemptuous of artistic "purity" won by willful disengagement or captured through the passive cruelty of indifference.

Between the poles of commitment and alienation Chekhov defined a way for himself which made him an artist *in the world*, independent of ideology but shunning as well the tempting vacuity of isolation. And he aimed to affect his world, not through propaganda or persuasion, but by giving his readers a heightened awareness of the quality of their lives: "A writer," he once said, "is not a little twittering bird. . . . If I live, think, fight and suffer, then all this is reflected in whatever I happen to write. I will describe

---

* Constance Garnett, ed. and trans., *Letters of Anton Chekhov to His Family and Friends* (New York: Macmillan, 1920). All quotations from the letters of Chekhov cited within the text as *Letters*, refer to this edition.

life to you truthfully, that is, artistically, and you will see in it what you have not seen before . . ." [6] Again, speaking of his plays—but what he says is equally true of his stories—Chekhov was even more direct about his purposes:

> All I wanted was to say honestly to people: "Have a look at yourselves and see how bad and dreary your lives are!" The important thing is that people should realize that, for when they do, they will most certainly create another and better life for themselves. I will not live to see it, but I know that it will be quite different, quite unlike our present life. And so long as this different life does not exist, I shall go on saying to people again and again: "Please, understand that your life is bad and dreary!" [7]

And David Magarshack, employing the imagery of Chekhov's story "Gooseberries," writes of him: "The man with a hammer in his hand knocking at the conscience of mankind —that was what Chekhov conceived the role of the creative writer to be, and that was what he conceived his own role as a writer to be, which is the very opposite of a fatalistic acceptance of things as they are." [8]

For Chekhov, though, this synthesis of artistic and social purposes was far from easy, and his progress toward it is an analogue of the progression in his writing. The years 1889-1892 were crucial in his metamorphosis from a popular writer of humorous tales and anecdotes into a serious artist of social consequence and purpose. At first, he felt only an inchoate discontent with his life and with a success which he often thought was all too easy and unmerited:

> I have not enough passion; [he wrote on May 4, 1889] add to that this sort of lunacy: for the last two years I have for no reason at all ceased to care about seeing my work in print, have become indifferent to reviews, to literary conversations, to gossip, to success and failure, to good pay—in short, I have gone downright silly.

There is a sort of stagnation in my soul. (*Letters*, p. 122)

But how little this malaise was merely "silly" can be felt in the bitterly nihilistic tone which suffuses Chekhov's only major work of 1889, "A Boring Story." Of course, one shouldn't equate Chekhov himself with the central figure of the story, but the correlations between his own feelings and the pain the story dramatizes are too marked to be merely accidental. And when the dying Professor in "A Boring Story" is finally confronted with the anguished demand of his stepdaughter, the only person for whom he really cares, that from the height of his intellect and detachment he give her an "answer" to lend some meaning to the futility and despair of her life, he can only confess his own emptiness: "I'm sorry, I can't tell you anything . . . Honestly, Katya, I don't know . . ." and he meditates on the lack in himself of "a ruling idea." [9]

Chekhov must have been feeling at this time the same sort of emptiness and waste of spirit that characterizes the Professor and become painfully conscious of the inadequacy of his own austere objectivity, when confronted with real human need. He always made a good deal of his medical training (Chekhov was also a physician), and of the realism into which science had trained him. But science, he found, was a habit of mind, not a scheme of values, and beyond the reach of its dependable procedures his emptiness remained. In 1892, when he had more fully formulated his discontent, Chekhov wrote to his friend, Suvorin:

Science and technical knowledge are passing through a great period now, but for our sort [the writers and artists of the age] it is a flabby, stale, and dull time. We are stale and dull ourselves, . . . The causes of this are not to be found in our stupidity, our lack of talent, or our insolence, . . . but in a disease which for the artist is worse than syphilis or sexual exhaustion. We lack "something," that is true, and that means that, lift the robe of our muse, and you will find within an empty void. . . . We paint life as it is, but beyond that—nothing at all. . . . Flog us and we can do no more! We have neither immediate nor remote aims, and in our soul there is a great empty space. We have no politics, we do not believe in revolution, we have no God, we are not afraid of ghosts, and I personally am not afraid even of death and blindness. One who wants nothing, hopes for nothing, and fears nothing, cannot be an artist. . . . Grigorovitch [an older writer who had encouraged Chekhov] and you think I am clever. Yes, I am at least so far clever as not to conceal from myself my disease, and not to deceive myself, and not to cover up my own emptiness with other people's rags, such as the ideas of the sixties, . . . (*Letters*, pp. 319-320)

Doubtless there were also many personal causes for Chekhov's frustration: he was continually involved in financial struggles and constantly in debt, as he was improvident, and besides, his father was a bankrupt and Chekhov had to support his large family; his health was poor, and the death of his older brother, Nicholas, from consumption in June of 1889 had shocked him into an awareness of the seriousness of his own tuberculosis; and he felt deeply the lack of fulfillment in his life, and the loneliness, from his not at that time loving and being loved by a woman. (Magarshack places great emphasis on Chekhov's unfulfilled love of a married woman, Lydia Avilov, a love which he felt passionately but to which his scruples were an insurmountable barrier.[10] But later Chekhov did marry happily.)

These factors were important, but there is no reason either to doubt Chekhov's repeated assertions that a primary source of his discontent was his sense of dissatisfaction with his situation as a writer and his identity as a citizen—and especially with the fact that he could not conjoin the two. Chekhov felt this frustration deeply—this want of "something"—and success could not compensate for it. Clearly, he had either to try to accept his alienation—perhaps ending in suicide, the ultimate acceptance, like Treplev in *The Seagull*—or find a new synthesis. Facing his discontent in its starkest terms, Chekhov saw that he had no real choice: he had to create an identity for himself that would enable him to be whole and effectual, both as artist and man, and to overcome the self-division he felt from the lack of coherence between his two roles.

Chekhov's response to his crisis was characteristic, both in its concreteness and in its *apparent* pointlessness. It was to depart, in April 1890, on a terribly arduous journey across nearly the whole of Russia to visit the penal colony on the island of Sakhalin. This adventure seemed to everyone willful and needless—and for a man in Chekhov's precarious health almost mad—and his family and friends tried vainly to talk him out of it. Why do this? everyone asked, and they could make little sense of his answers. Perhaps, though, they did not take seriously enough the reasons he gave:

> . . . you [Suvorin] say that Sahalin [*sic*] is of no use and no interest to anyone. Can that be true? Sahalin can be useless and uninteresting only to a society which does not exile thousands of people to it and does not spend millions of roubles on it. . . . Sahalin is a place of the most unbearable sufferings of which man, free and captive, is capable. . . . I am not sentimental, or I would say that we ought to go to places like Sahalin to worship as the Turks go to Mecca, and that sailors and gaolers ought to think of the prison in Sahalin as military men think of Sevastopol. . . . It is evident that we have sent *millions* of men to rot in prison, have destroyed them—casually, without thinking, barbarously; we have driven men in fetters, through the cold ten thousand versts, have infected them with syphilis, have

depraved them, have multiplied criminals, and the blame for all this we have thrown upon the gaolers and red-nosed superintendents. Now all educated Europe knows that it is not the superintendents that are to blame, but all of us; yet that has nothing to do with us, it is not interesting. (*Letters*, pp. 133-134)

For Chekhov the journey to Sakhalin, including the research done there (his book *The Island of Sakhalin* appeared about three years later and was helpful in furthering reforms on the island), was neither improbable nor irrational—nor was it merely an "escape." It was an act of conscience, his personal witness against the unthinking cruelty of his society. By it, Chekhov broke the shell of his alienation and liberated his conscience. And in it he established his *ethos,* his standing to be a "critic" of his society, so that he could function in a larger, more consequential way than he had—as an artist who was also a citizen of his state, and of the world.

"Chekhov," writes Magarshack, "returned a different man from Sakhalin, and his journey to that Island of Lost Souls was in reality a pilgrimage in search of his own soul, though he may not have realized it at the time." [11] But he must have known, intuitively perhaps, that the sort of spiritual emptiness embodied in "A Boring Story" and recurrent in his letters demanded more than an intellectual awareness, and that compassion would only be another evasion unless it was effectual and purposive. His demon could only be exorcised in action and engagement. And the right to this, and the power to be effective, had to be *earned* in a very basic and simple way—by risking not only one's money or fame but also one's body and health, life itself if it came to that. A very "Christian" standpoint, though Chekhov was not a believer in any formal sense.

Thus, in the years 1889-1892, Chekhov created his consciousness and defined his particular, artist's connection with his reality. This connection was not primarily intellectual and not at all ideological: Chekhov was only confirmed in his disenchantment with systems and programs, especially Tolstoy's, by seeing how little they could matter on Sakhalin.[12] His engagement was *humane,* in the deepest, most basic sense. He had a great gift of response, which was concrete and direct, never filtered through abstractions, and the human being was always at the center of his vision —the "real" person, not a sentimentalized or idealized concept which only converted men, by the duress of a compulsive definition of human nature, into debating points for a philosophy. "People must never be humiliated—," he wrote, "that is the main thing." [13] It also became "the main thing" in his art.

Alexander Kuprin writes, in his "Reminiscences" of Chekhov, that at the core of his being was "the agony of an exceptionally refined, charming, and sensitive soul, who suffered beyond measure from banality, coarseness, dreariness, nothingness, violence, savagery—the whole horror and darkness of modern everyday existence." [14] But Chekhov was no passive sufferer, nor did he isolate himself in his pain. His suffering was an index of his responsiveness, of his "interest" in his world and in the quality of other men's lives. And his resolution of his personal crisis of 1889-1892 brought him to a place where, contending against the seductive temptation of insularity as well as against the too-easy gratification of commitment to a program, he was able to make his "agony" the action of his works. As Maxim Gorky writes:

> He was ingeniously shy, he would not say aloud and openly to people: "Now do be more decent"; he hoped in vain that they would themselves see how necessary it was that they should be more decent. He hated everything banal and foul, and he described the abominations of life in the noble language of a poet, with the

humorist's gentle smile, and behind the beautiful form of his stories people scarcely noticed the inner meaning, full of bitter reproach.[15]

"Ward No. 6" was the first important result of Chekhov's new purposiveness, and of all his "bitter reproaches" it is perhaps the most intense. "A Boring Story" was less a reproach than a cry of despair, which did not lead much beyond its own pain. But by the time of "Ward No. 6" despair has been quelled, and the pain is armed. Later Chekhov's humor would reassert itself, though usually ironically, and melancholy would soften his anger. But in 1892, when he wrote this story under the full impact of Sakhalin, the thrust of his attack is uncompromising. As Sakhalin typified for Chekhov the thoughtless barbarousness of his world, Ward No. 6 was its microcosm, not its "symbol." The story's relevance and point is not metaphorical but concrete. There was no need to grope for grander, metaphysically richer metaphors to embody what Gorky calls "the abominations of life": reality was abominable enough.

# III

"Ward No. 6," especially in terms of its contextual resonances, is essentially a work of anger and condemnation. There is no resignation in it, no elegy for the dying world, no consolation, but on the contrary an agonized awareness of decay and a bitter indictment of those who, by their sloth, thoughtlessness, and cowardice, collaborate in their own destruction and the destruction of other men.

The story centrally concerns Dr. Andrei Yefimich Ragin, a slothful provincial physician in charge of a decrepit hospital, which has an annex reserved for the "insane" called Ward No. 6. Ivan Dimitrich Gromov, a patient in Ward No. 6, exerts a compelling fascination on Dr. Ragin who, through his relationship with Ivan, comes to realize the full horror of Ward No. 6 and his own complicity in this cruelty. Fully conscious for the first time, Dr. Ragin rapidly disintegrates under the pressure of his new knowledge, ending an inmate of Ward No. 6 himself, and dying finally in a bitter agony of pain and frustration.

Tolstoy's Ivan Ilych, pressed finally to simplicity by the inevitability of his death, does find an answer and is able to build some consolation out of the ultimate consciousness of the waste of his life. "Ward No. 6," written in the flood of Chekhov's anti-Tolstoyan reaction, is almost an "answer" to "The Death of Ivan Ilych." Dr. Ragin's final understanding of his life holds no consolation, only terror at the cruelty of his lifelong obtuseness, and his death is no release but as meaningless and futile as his life:

> He bit the pillow and clenched his teeth with pain, and suddenly amid the chaos, the terrible unendurable thought flashed clearly in his mind that these people who now looked like black shadows in the moonlight must have experienced the same pain for years, day after day. How could it happen that throughout over twenty years he had not known and had not wanted to know that? He had not known, had had no understanding of pain, meaning he was not guilty, yet his conscience, as intractable and hard as Nikita, made him grow cold from the top of his head to his heels. He jumped up, wanted to cry out with all his strength and run as fast as possible to kill Nikita, then Khobotov, the superintendent, and the orderly, then himself, but not a sound came out of his chest and his legs would not obey; panting, he tore at the bathrobe and shirt over his chest, ripped them, and fell unconscious on the bed. (p. 156)*

---

* *Seven Short Novels of Chekhov*, trans. Barbara Makanowitzky (New York: Bantam Books, 1963). All quotations from "Ward No. 6," cited within the text only by page numbers, refer to this edition.

And only some seventeen lines later comes the announcement of his death.

Chekhov portrays the stages in Dr. Ragin's disintegration with an almost clinical severity. But his is ultimately a fall more terrible and moving even than the agony of his *alter ego,* Ivan Dimitrich, whose trouble, as Ivan himself recognizes, is *only* a "persecution complex." Dr. Ragin's "case" is more paradoxical: his deterioration runs parallel to his growing awareness and is a logical complement of his new capacity of feeling. And this consciousness, ironically, comes too late and cannot be realized in action—not even in the sort of symbolic gesture of acquiescence that Ivan Ilych is able to make—but can only burn in the impotent panic of a horror which is sane enough, at long last, to seem mad, a "complex" rooted in the unendurable recognition of *himself* as a "persecutor." (If it is strong, the truth may indeed "make you free," but if it is powerless, it is more likely to imprison you.)

Dr. Ragin, then, is forced to a confrontation of himself and of the cruelty inherent in his indifference. This is a cruelty of irresponsibility more subtle than Nikita's violence, that destroys "casually, without thinking, barbarously," as Chekhov put it in speaking of Sakhalin. Chekhov is ironical to the end, though, and Dr. Ragin's confrontation of himself is not complete: even at the last extremity he wants to evade the personal responsibility for his guilt by pleading his ignorance as mitigation, though the harsh reality of his situation will not let the rationalization hold then.

But Chekhov's irony is proof against *his reader's* evasion, and surely he wants to force the same kind of confrontation —with no compromise—in *them.* His basic rhetorical strategy is built on the thematic fulcrum of the "double": the central figure's identification with another man who becomes his mirror, reflecting his character, imaging his flaws, and by the force of his being compelling him to self-knowledge. (This is the same sort of action that is working

in Conrad's "The Secret Sharer," for instance, or in Mann's "Death in Venice," or at the end in Henry James's "The Beast in the Jungle.") And Dr. Ragin is a "double," in his turn, for all the men of his class and with his sort of ineptitude, a slothful inhumanity so deep and so consequential—so criminal, in fact—that Chekhov wants it identified as an *evil* so that responsibility for its effects cannot be evaded, or excused, or rationalized as social inevitability.

There is nothing "inevitable" about Dr. Ragin's downfall, regardless of his own self-exculpating illusions. He is no victim, nor is his story tragic. To begin with, he is a man of some competence and good will. But the dull, futile existence of a provincial doctor—the banality and cupidity of his life and the life around him—quickly enervates him. He sinks, not by design but through inertia, into a hermetic, pseudo-intellectual isolation, making no effort either to be an effective physician or to correct the rank abuses it is in his power to ameliorate. In his weakness, he allows his hospital to fall deeper and deeper into its "terrible state," failing to attend even to Ward No. 6, where conditions are worst of all:

> There is probably no place on earth where life is as monotonous as in the annex. In the mornings, the patients, except for the paralytic and the fat peasant, wash in the entry in a big tub and dry themselves with the tails of their bathrobes; after that they drink tea brought by Nikita from the main building in tin mugs; each is entitled to one mugful. At noon they eat *kasha* and sour cabbage soup; in the evening they sup on the *kasha* left over from dinner. In the intervals they lie, sleep, look out the window, and pace the room. And so on every day. (pp. 116-117)

And of course no one among these forgotten people is ever cured, for the only "care" is the punishment inflicted by Nikita, the keeper, whose brutality is only a commitment to "order" slavishly enacted, in which the psychology of Russian autocracy is satirized.

But the heart of Dr. Ragin's criminality is not merely that he is obtuse and ineffectual but that he is dishonest in rationalizing his own ineptitude. And this sort of hypocrisy is also the core of Chekhov's quarrel with his society.

In his more perceptive moments Dr. Ragin knows very well that he is a fraud: "I serve a pernicious business and receive a salary from people I swindle; I'm dishonest." But immediately comes the evasion:

> "But, of course, I'm nothing by myself, I'm only a part of an inevitable social evil: all provincial officials are harmful and receive salaries for nothing. . . . Meaning it's not I who am guilty in my dishonesty, but the times. . . . If I had been born two hundred years later, I would be another person." (p. 127)

Typical of the "intelligentsia" of his day, Dr. Ragin's thin layer of sophistication is his curse. By using his "ideas" sophistically, he continually evades his personal responsibility and narcotizes whatever conscience he might have had by weaving a protective insulation for himself out of the intellectual remnants of the age. And since he is too lazy really to think originally, he converts any thought he touches, though it might have been respectable in itself, into a lie by his use of it.

Dr. Ragin's "philosophy" is a hodgepodge of second-hand, counterfeit wisdom: philosophical long views—"prejudices and all life's filth and foulness were needed because they would be transformed into something useful with the passage of time, just as manure becomes rich soil" (p. 119); religious fatalism—"why keep people from dying if death is the normal, legitimate end for everyone? . . . suffering is said to lead man to perfection, . . . if humanity does, in fact, learn to alleviate its sufferings with drops and pills, it will completely cast aside religion and philosophy, in which it has found until now not just a defense against all kinds of ills, but even happiness" (p. 120); romantic idealism—"'everything in the world is insignificant and uninteresting except the high spiritual manifestations of the human mind'" (p. 123); romantic pessimism—"'Life is an exasperating trap'" (p. 124); and so forth.

Dr. Ragin's image of himself is unreal and "literary" in a way that is like Madame Bovary's compulsive self-deception. He sees himself in terms of the typical "hero" of later nineteenth-century Russian literature: a "superfluous man." Berlin describes the "type" in this way:

> . . . the prototype of many a Russian Hamlet, too idealistic and too honest to accept the squalor and the lies of conventional society, too weak and too civilized to work effectively for their destruction, and consequently displaced from his proper function and doomed to poison his own life and the lives of others by neurotic behaviour induced by the vices of a society which sins against the moral ideals which the author holds dear—either irremediably corrupt, or still capable of regeneration, according to the author's social or religious beliefs.[16]

In "Ward No. 6," Chekhov not only works a variation on the type of the "superfluous man" but, more importantly, looks beyond the type at the writers and intellectuals who created it. By illuminating the type's essential hollowness, the quasi-romantic evasion at its core, Chekhov indicts its creators' irresponsibility and challenges both the pessimism and the messianism of which Berlin speaks. Thus, he moves beyond Flaubert's sort of aesthetical disdain into a concerned involvement and social criticism.

This was not the first time that Chekhov had undertaken this sort of character; he was continually fascinated by the problems it presented. In 1887, in his play *Ivanov,* he had made his first major assault on the type. (His early, self-suppressed play *Platonov* is essentially a study for *Ivanov*.) Ivanov's character is neurotic, keyed around the concept of "premature exhaustion," as is Dr. Ragin's. But Chekhov tends to take Ivanov seriously, not ironically, even fashioning him a cut above the type:

> Conscious of physical exhaustion and boredom, he does not understand what is the matter with him, and what has happened. . . . Finding themselves in such a position, narrow and unconscientious people generally throw the whole blame on their environment, or write themselves down as Hamlets and superfluous people, and are satisfied with that. But Ivanov, a straightforward man, openly says . . . that he does not understand his own mind. "I don't understand! I don't understand!" (*Letters,* pp. 112-113)

Ivanov is obtuse but he is at least honest, and Chekhov is ambivalent about him, sometimes even seeming to identify with Ivanov's confusion and ennui in spite of his critical intentions.

Chekhov had intended *Ivanov* to be an *exposé* of the literary type of the "superfluous man." But as he later understood, the play does not successfully realize this intention. Its failure to do so and its differences from "Ward No. 6" are instructive.

The problem in *Ivanov* is essentially that Chekhov has not yet quite decided what he thinks of the "superfluous man." He tries to work *within* the convention of the type, accepting its premises as legitimate, and at the same time to criticize it. Lacking an ironical standpoint toward Ivanov (and beset by structural problems in the drama that he had not yet solved[17]), Chekhov is trapped in a disjunction between aim and method. In another sense, Chekhov has not yet defined the *moral quality* of the type. Consequently, he is unable to show the *meaning* of Ivanov's character in terms of his effect on the field of social and human relationships in which he exists. Without this sort of "objectification" the evidence for judgment cannot emerge and criticism is disarmed. The problem in *Ivanov* arises from the fact that Chekhov is not yet looking through the type to judge its validity. Crediting it so far as to use the type as the representation of a possible human nature, his criticism is blunted against the artistic persuasiveness of his character, and insofar as Ivanov is presented as an authentic person one is bound to sympathize with him. The type is seductive: if the writer takes it on its own terms and not from an ironical point of view, he is caught within the myth—negative intentions notwithstanding. To "use" is to be compromised.

The metamorphosis that Chekhov underwent between *Ivanov* and "Ward No. 6" developed in him the critical point of view that he lacked in 1887. In "Ward No. 6" he demonstrates that *the type itself* is an evasion which carries its own built-in apologia—the premise that the character's "superfluousness" is really no fault of his own, that the "Hamletlike" figure is somehow too good to cope with a diseased society. So long as this assumption is accepted as part of the definition of the type, no matter how much the writer wants to condemn his "typical" character, he carries, inherently, an unimpeachable *raison d'être*. But for Chekhov, in his time, the premise is invalid and the type a fraud. It may have been created originally as an honest attempt to *explain* a sort of personality—as, for example, Turgenev created his Rudin—but as it was exploited by people to develop a psychology of evasion, the type became less an explanation than a *justification* for their own ignorance and inhumanity. Chekhov's intention in "Ward No. 6" is to show this.

Not accepting any grandiose metaphysical or religious scheme of values such as Tolstoy or the messianic philosophers had—indeed wanting to contend against such patterns of thought—Chekhov had to create a context of judgment without extrahuman sanctions. (This is the old "humanist" dilemma, perhaps: he wants Christ without God.) Chekhov, thus, arms his own humane values of sympathy and intelligence—of "decency," in his own favorite term—by establishing the conventional "superfluous man" as a social being whose actions have consequences and whose internal evasions, regardless of their motivation, are manifest as crimes against himself and other men because they cause pain and suffering. In so doing, he tries to make contact with a responsiveness deeper than ideology, with an elemental, humane power of identification—the response to Christ on the cross that is independent of theology—to give the lie to ideology itself.

He does this by constantly showing Dr. Ragin within a field of social and physical realities, which contradict his "philosophy" and which ironically unmask the falsity, obtuseness, and self-deception at the heart of it. The force of these contradictions is such that even Dr. Ragin himself must eventually react to them, suffering the disintegration which leads to his downfall. And of course the greatest of these forces is his *alter ego,* Ivan Dimitrich, the "one interesting and remarkable mind". (p. 140) in the town, sick though he is. Ivan's "reason in madness" makes Dr. Ragin confront, without abstraction or evasion, a human pain and suffering which refutes his whole scheme of superhuman stoicism and reduces his sophistry to absurdity. Ivan Dimitrich's passionate response to life, his concrete, unsophisticated reality is the challenge Chekhov would hurl at his society's inhumanity, just as Ivan Dimitrich continually confronts Dr. Ragin with his pain:

"What's this you're telling me about Diogenes and about some kind of understanding?" He suddenly became angry and jumped up. "I love life, love it passionately! I have a persecution complex, a constantly tormenting fear, but there are minutes when a thirst for life seizes me, and then I am afraid of going out of my mind. I want terribly to live, terribly." (p. 131)

"Understanding . . ." frowned Ivan Dimitrich. "External, internal . . . I'm sorry, I don't understand it. All I know," he said, standing up and looking angrily at the doctor; "all I know is that God created me out of warm blood and nerves, yes! And organic tissue, if it's viable, must react to every irritation. And I react! I answer pain with a cry and tears; villainy with displeasure; foulness with revulsion. In my opinion this is reality and what is called life. The lower the organism, the less sensitive it is, and the more feebly it responds to irritation; the higher it is, the more responsively and energetically it reacts to reality. How could one deny that? A doctor, and he doesn't know such simple things." (pp. 134-135)

"A doctrine which teaches indifference to wealth and the comforts of life, contempt for suffering and death, [Stoicism] is absolutely incomprehensible to the large majority, because this majority has never known either wealth or comfort in life; and to despise suffering would mean to despise one's own life, for man's whole existence consists of the sensations of hunger, cold, insult, deprivation, and a Hamletlike fear of death. The whole of life lies in these sensations: one may be oppressed by it, hate it, but not despise it." (p. 135)

"And take Christ? Christ responded to reality by crying, smiling, grieving, growing angry; even feeling melancholy; He didn't go to meet sufferings with a smile and didn't have contempt for death, but prayed in the Garden of Gethsemane that this cup would pass Him by." (pp. 135-136)

Thus, Ivan Dimitrich's force of life, the power of his passion and suffering even in his madness, and his humanity expose the sham and cruelty of Dr. Ragin's disengaged sophistry. And, by extension, the type of the "superfluous man" is criticized—as are those who created it and those who "live the part."

The ultimate reversal of roles between the doubles, Dr. Ragin's own "insanity" and incarceration, does not come about because Chekhov wants to weave Pirandelloesque paradoxes about the chimeric distinction between "sanity" and "insanity." Besides the structural "rightness" of it, he wants to clinch his argument against the Tolstoyan ethic of nonresistance to evil and against "religious" unworldliness generally. Tolstoy's morality is no evasion as is the type of the "superfluous man," but to Chekhov it is just as unrealistic and ineffectual. In Dr. Ragin's impotence after his discovery of the truth Chekhov ironically images "nonresistance." Another sort of unworldliness was Dostoyevsky's more mystical variety, and Chekhov seemed to find this much more harmful. Dostoyevsky once wrote: "The strongest, most fundamental need of the Russian people is the need of suffering, continual suffering, everywhere and in everything." [18] Some of Dr. Ragin's "philosophical" opinions sound almost like a parody of Dostoyevsky's crypto-Christianity.

In essence, it can be seen that the primary drive of "Ward No. 6" as it coheres with its world is Chekhov's desire to expose the inhumanity and ridicule the sophistry of a number of kinds of evasiveness and passivity which were blind to the actualities of Russian life. Chekhov is very concrete. He regards the intellectualizing, or abstracting, or spiritualizing of social problems as forms of self-deception—a terrible danger in intelligence that could block the basic, nonintellectual humane response to suffering and baseness by insulating a man's conscience with theory, or ratiocination, or theology. The deception could be merely obtuse or sophistical, as is Dr. Ragin's "superfluousness"; it could be abstracted in its messianism, as in varying ways were Tolstoy's and Dostoyevsky's religiousness; it could be simply vulgar and ignorant, as is Nikita's violence and the cruelty of the society around him of which his brutality is only the unmasked representation. In any form it is blind to the realities of its world, and in its blindness is *de facto* evil.

Chekhov catches these "realities" in the sense of oppression, the feeling of confinement and meaninglessness, that permeates "Ward No. 6" and points out the mindless inhumanity of his society. He is pessimistic and despite his occasional "lighter" moments—such as Ivan Dimitrich's perfervid visions of the future—seems to have little hope for his world; as Edmund Wilson says: "One of the strongest impressions, in fact, conveyed by the whole of Chekhov's work is that, although the old order is petering out, there is not very much to build on for a sound democratic and up-to-date Russia." [19] But Chekhov allows neither his realism nor his skepticism to inhibit his humanity and, after conquering the alienation of 1889-1892, his morality was "to face"—as he had faced the horrors of Sakhalin—and to tell the truth in art to his world, to make it "face" too if he could.

In that his realism was essentially hopeless, Chekhov's honesty is all the more courageous. Though he is never polemical or "prophetic," and constitutionally he simply *could not be* didactic or censorious, Chekhov's humanist ethic is pervasive in its force. Robert Brustein is, I think, more perceptive than most critics in characterizing this special quality:

> . . . Chekhov's impersonality is a surface characteristic; and beneath this surface is a satiric, admonitory moralist, . . . Chekhov the realist pretends to have no other aim than the faithful representation of reality; but Chekhov the moralist is always conscious of a higher purpose than mere imitation. . . . Chekhov, in short, "observes, chooses, guesses, combines" [quoting from an 1888 letter of Chekhov's] for a special purpose—not to

remedy particular evils but to represent them accurately —and it is through this representation that he exercises, indirectly, the moral function of his art.[20]

The anger and force of "Ward No. 6" is its "meaning" and its "being" (to play with MacLeish's terminology). The story is transactional, not discrete: it lives in its connections with the concrete human situation out of which it emerges and with the social and intellectual forces with which it deals, and it has little of the rarefied "beauty" we often tend to associate with art. The story is fully engaged with the life around it; it is *inherently*—not contentiously—critical and judgmental. It exists most vitally in the humaneness which actuates and suffuses it. And its dimension and force can only be clearly seen in terms of the story's relationships with its context.

In the quality of his literary involvement Chekhov emerges from a long-standing tradition in Russia, which began, roughly, in the first half of the nineteenth century with the critic Belinsky. Of him, Nicolas Berdyaev has written: "Above all, Belinsky . . . rebels against an abstract idealism remote from concrete life, which sacrifices the individual to the general, the living human person to the world soul. 'The fate of the subject, the individual, the person,' he writes, 'is more important than the fate of the whole world or the well-being of the Chinese Emperor.' "[21] Belinsky, I should think, would have approved of "Ward No. 6."

# IV

Whether the style of "contextual" criticism advocated here is generally workable and worth the time in "research" that it takes—even if it *really* is criticism—are still open questions. Many literary theorists have inveighed against extrinsic criticism from structural or formalist positions as an attitude which takes one not toward but away from the particular literary work, into rhetoric or philosophy. And the force of such objections must be admitted: what point is there in studying around and about a work, when you should be concentrating on the work itself?

Still, similar objections might be leveled against almost any kind of criticism. None of it, "intrinsic" or not, *is* the poem. The ideal situation, surely, is to let each reader alone to discover the literary work for himself and come to his own best terms with it. But so long as most of us are imperfect, our time is limited, and we do admit that there may be some point in criticism—in the work of more knowledgeable heads than the "common reader," which may help the individual by offering him insights he normally would not possess—what good reason is there for barring any sort of approach which can indeed offer such insight?

Those who would be exclusive in criticism usually end by creating a theory which, if argued to its logical extreme, would undermine the rationale of all criticism—even their own specialty. True, contextual criticism may go wrong, but so may any critical viewpoint. The only valid measure still is in the results, and many brilliant examples of extrinsic criticism prove that such approaches are no more inherently unsound, or unliterary, than other ways of criticism. Conceiving of the literary work in a larger way than intrinsic criticism does, the extrinsic critic would decline the self-conscious role assigned him by his detractors. His modes of analysis and his insights, he would feel, are just as relevant, just as meaningful, as the intrinsic critic's more limited thinking.

The specific relevance of contextual criticism for the oral interpreter is a more complex question. The first answer that comes to mind is the obvious one: the oral interpreter is interested in achieving the fullest possible apprehension of the literary work, and *any* style of criticism which can help him in this is per se justifiable.

But in a less obvious sense, there is a more specific relevance for the oral interpreter in this kind of critical thinking. The interpreter's special mode of literary study has its crux in his reconstituting the work of literature as performance, making the writer's "symbolic act" momentarily his own action too by his reënacting of it. And in this, it is hoped, he will come to know the work deeply and meaningfully—perhaps *more* deeply and meaningfully than he could usually know it by more abstract styles of analysis. Thus, for the interpreter, performance is less an end than a means, less a completed establishment of sounds and gestures than a crucible in which his intelligence of the work is always in flux, constantly being tempered.

In this the interpreter, of necessity, pushes all literary forms toward the "dramatic": he is a voice, and body, and mind that are *present,* that are there; his time is always *now,* his act is always immediate; he is a *person,* not a "text," not a communicative machine. I don't mean to suggest that the interpreter always creates "drama" in any formal sense, but that the concreteness and personality of his *presence,* as the embodiment of the work, creates, *prima facie,* a quasi-dramatic situation in which something must "happen"—his intelligence and skill must make the work *live,* or performance would be pointless.

If all this is true, the very nature of what the oral interpreter does works against detachment or aestheticism and toward his taking an experiential, engaged tack with the work. By virtue of his being and presence he makes the literary work take on this concrete life as well. Thus, the style of criticism suggested here is, in fact, *more* relevant for the interpreter than it is for any other sort of reader. The interpreter *must* conceive of the literary work as "action" and define its meaning in these terms. For him to find the tone, the stance, the motive of the work, he would have to feel it as alive and purposive, real and immanent in its context which, for the sake of performance, must temporarily become his context too.

In the case of "Ward No. 6," for example, for the oral

interpreter to limit his analysis to the intrinsic might have some serious consequences that would be felt in performance: his "attack" might not be right—taking too abstract a hold on the story, he might tend to lose the force of its purposive, realistic strength and to soften it so that Chekhov seemed merely sadly resigned, not engaged and critical as he was. This would be, in effect, to do much the same thing for which Dr. Ragin is indicted and what Chekhov's appreciators have too often done—"roll onto their backs and purr." If he did this, the interpreter would sacrifice the great advantage inherent in his medium—its way of testing his truthfulness and refining his apprehension of the work through the necessity of "action." And I think he would sacrifice a good deal of the meaning of the story as well, diminishing its essential force, compromising its authority, making impure what Chekhov liked to call the "iron" in the blood.

NOTES

1. George Steiner, *Tolstoy or Dostoevsky* (New York: Vintage, 1961), p. 6.
2. This is the subtitle of her book. Princess Nina Andronikova Toumanova, *Anton Chekhov* (New York: Columbia University Press, 1960).
3. Irving Howe, *Politics and the Novel* (New York: Meridian, 1957), p. 120.
4. Constance Garnett, ed. and trans., *Letters of Anton Chekhov to His Family and Friends* (New York: Macmillan, 1920), pp. 55-59, 88-89, 99-100, 141.
5. "Introduction" to Alexander Herzen, *From the Other Shore and The Russian People and Socialism* (Cleveland: Meridian, 1963), p. xvii.

6. Quoted in David Magarshack, *Chekhov: A Life* (New York: Grove, 1952), p. 173.
7. Quoted in David Magarshack, *Chekhov the Dramatist* (New York: Dramabooks, 1960), p. 14.
8. *Chekhov: A Life*, p. 327.
9. *Lady with Lapdog and other Stories,* trans. David Magarshack (Baltimore: Penguin, 1964), p. 103.
10. *Chekhov: A Life*, pp. 174-175.
11. *Chekhov: A Life*, p. 176.
12. *Chekhov: A Life*, pp. 175-176, 216.
13. Quoted in *Chekhov: A Life*, p. 18.
14. Alexander Kuprin, "Reminiscences of Anton Tchekhov," in S. S. Koteliansky, ed. and trans., *Anton Tchekhov: Literary and Theatrical Reminiscences* (London: Routledge, 1927), p. 52.
15. Maxim Gorky, *Reminiscences of Tolstoy, Chekhov, and Andreyev* (New York: Compass, 1959), p. 82.
16. "Introduction" to *From the Other Shore and The Russian People and Socialism*, p. ix.
17. See Magarshack, *Chekhov the Dramatist*.
18. Quoted in E. H. Carr, *Dostoevsky, 1821-1881* (New York: Barnes & Noble, 1963), p. 223.
19. "Preface" to Anton Chekhov, *Peasants and other Stories* (Garden City, N.Y.: Anchor, 1956), p. x.
20. Robert Brustein, *The Theatre of Revolt* (Boston: Little, Brown, 1964), p. 147.
21. Nicholas Berdayev, *The Origin of Russian Communism* (Ann Arbor, Mich.: Ann Arbor Paperbacks, 1960), pp. 39-40.

RECOMMENDED READING

Chekhov's stories and plays are available in many editions. The Constance Garnett edition of his letters is difficult to find now, but happily a good selection of Chekhov's letters has recently been reprinted: Louis S. Friedland, ed., *Letters on the Short Story, the Drama and other Literary Topics* (New York: Benjamin Blom, 1964).

Other valuable studies of Chekhov in addition to the critical and biographical works cited in the body of the essay are: two works by W. H. Bruford, *Chekhov* (New Haven: Yale University Press, 1957) and *Chekhov and His Russia* (New York: Oxford University Press, 1948); Ernest J. Simmons, *Chekhov* (Boston: Little, Brown, 1962); and the more general literary histories of Marc Slonim, which include a number of segments on Chekhov, *From Chekhov to the Revolution* (New York: Galaxy, 1962) and *Russian Theatre* (New York: Collier, 1962). Randall Jarrell's "Introduction" to "Ward No. 6" in *Six Russian Short Novels* (Garden City, N. Y.: Anchor, 1963) explores many fine insights within a short compass and suggests a standpoint toward the story that is similar to that employed in this essay.

The "intrinsic-extrinsic" formulation I have used is taken from Wayne Shumaker's study, *Elements of Critical Theory* (Berkeley: University of California Press, 1952), to which I am indebted. Other valuable works in literary theory, which approach the question of critical partitions from various perspectives, are: Northrop Frye, *Anatomy of Criticism* (Princeton, N.J.: Princeton University Press, 1957); Theodore M. Greene, *The Arts and the Art of Criticism* (Princeton, N.J.: Princeton University Press, 1940); Stanley Edgar Hyman, *The Armed Vision* (New York: Knopf, 1952); Herbert J. Muller, *Science and Criticism* (New York: George Braziller, 1956); Stephen C. Pepper, *The Basis of Criticism in the Arts* (Cambridge, Mass.: Harvard University Press, 1949); and René Welleck and Austin Warren, *Theory of Literature,* 3rd ed. (New York: Harvest, 1963).

Kenneth Burke's writing is extremely diverse and rather cryptic; his work is most readily available in: *A Grammar of Motives* (New York: Prentice-Hall, 1945), *A Rhetoric of Motives* (New York: Prentice-Hall, 1950), and *The Philosophy of Literary Form* (New York: Vintage, 1957). William H. Reuckert, *Kenneth Burke and the Drama of Human Relations* (Minneapolis: University of Minnesota Press, 1963) is an excellent exegesis of Burke's theories. From the standpoint of this essay R. P. Blackmur's most pertinent works are: *Eleven Essays in the European Novel* (New York: Harbinger, 1964) and *The Lion and the Honeycomb* (New York: Harcourt, Brace, 1955).

The question of the writer's relationship to the world in which he lives has always been a vexing problem. It has been considered profoundly in: Joyce Cary, *Art and Reality* (New York: Harper, 1958); Jean-Paul Sartre, *What Is Literature?* (New York: Philosophical Library, 1949); and in various writings of Camus, Coleridge, Mann, Plato, Tolstoy, and many others.

Howe's *Politics and the Novel* (see note 3 above) is a truly basic extrinsic critical study. Other critical works which have been successful in working, more or less, from extrinsic standpoints are: Eric Bentley, *The Playwright as Thinker* (New York: Harcourt, Brace, 1946); Leslie Fiedler, *An End to Innocence* (Boston: Beacon Press, 1955); Erich Heller, *The Disinherited Mind* (New York: Meridian, 1959); R. W. B. Lewis, *The American Adam* (Chicago: Phoenix, 1955); Georg Lukács, *Studies in European Realism* (New York: University Library, 1964); Norman Podhoretz, *Doings and Undoings* (New York: Farrar, Straus, 1964); Philip Rahv, *Image and Idea* (Norfolk, Conn.: New Directions, 1957); Mark Schorer, *Sinclair Lewis* (New York: McGraw-Hill Book Co., 1961); Wylie Sypher, *Loss of the Self in Modern Literature and Art* (New York: Random House, 1962); Lionel Trilling, *The Liberal Imagination* (Garden City, N.Y.: Anchor, 1954); and Edmund Wilson, *Patriotic Gore* (New York: Oxford, 1962).

## *Projects*

The following projects may be used as the bases for short papers analyzing selections to be read aloud in class. Stories and poems in projects 3, 4, 5, and 6 may be found in Milton Crane, ed., *Fifty Great Short Stories* (New York: Bantam, 1952) and Oscar Williams, ed., *Immortal Poems of the English Language* (New York: Washington Square, 1952).

1. Gleb Struve, in his Preface to "Ward No. 6" in the Makanowitzky volume (quoted from in this chapter), denies that Chekhov himself would probably have thought of the Ward as a "microcosm" of Russian society. Thus, he would seem to undermine the point of view of this chapter from its inception. But is this a real difference, or only one of terminology? And if the disagreement *does* have substance, do you feel that this chapter makes a good argument for its point of view? (Assuming, of course, that none of us can *really* know what Chekhov intended.)

2. Tolstoy often criticized Chekhov for lacking a dominating idea or principle. Judging from a story such as "My Life" or "Peasants," do you think this is a valid criticism? If so, is it a *negative* point, as Tolstoy saw it? *Should* a writer work under the sway of such a dominating idea?

3. Consider James Joyce's story "Ivy Day in the Committee Room" as a response to post-Revolutionary Ireland. Who was Parnell? How does Joyce react to Irish "democracy"? How deep, or bitter, is Joyce's irony about the state of his nation?

4. William Faulkner was doubtless a Southerner to the core. But he was also an artist and felt obliged, first of all, to the truth of his experience. The "truth," though, for a contemporary, conscious Southerner, is a tense, ambiguous thing. How does Faulkner's "That Evening Sun" reflect the agony of a man torn between the values of a tradi-

tional culture he loves and the humane values that are individually his? How does the story image the terrible ambivalence of the Southerner toward the Negro?

5. Consider W. H. Auden's poem "September 1, 1939" as a response to the events of that day and an attempt to come to terms with its terrible realities. What happened on September 1, 1939? How much real affirmation is there in the poet's desire to "show an affirming flame"? In the situation he describes how is this possible?

6. F. T. Prince's poem "Soldiers Bathing" is very concrete in its manipulation of the setting of war but ambiguous in what the poet finally comes to about this reality. Does the poet resolve the tension between Christianity and war? *Can* it be "resolved," or is the ambiguity of paradox his only alternative?

# INDEX

# Index